60 Campsite Reviews plus tips on
PACKING ▲ CAMP COOKING ▲ FESTIVALS

Camping
RECORD BOOK

SARAH ALEXANDER

In loving memory of Val Coulcher
My camping inspiration

First published 2010

The History Press
The Mill, Brimscombe Port
Stroud, Gloucestershire, GL5 2QG
www.thehistorypress.co.uk

© Sarah Alexander, 2010

The right of Sarah Alexander to be identified as the Author
of this work has been asserted in accordance with the
Copyrights, Designs and Patents Act 1988.

All rights reserved. No part of this book may be reprinted
or reproduced or utilised in any form or by any electronic,
mechanical or other means, now known or hereafter invented,
including photocopying and recording, or in any information
storage or retrieval system, without the permission in writing
from the Publishers.

British Library Cataloguing in Publication Data.
A catalogue record for this book is available from the British Library.

ISBN 978 0 7524 5712 3

Typesetting and origination by The History Press
Printed in italy

Perfect Pitch
the online camping magazine

Cover: © ScotImage/Alamy
All other images from iStockphoto except
p.27 courtesy of Hole Station Campsite; p.31
courtesy of Yurt Camp Devon; p.34 courtesy
of Thistledown Centre; p.39 courtesy of
Bryher Campsite; p.48 courtesy of Manor
Court Farm; p.53 courtesy of Hidden Spring
Vineyard; p.56 courtesy of Croft Cottage
Camping; p. 68 courtesy of Foxholes Castle
Camping; p.73 courtesy of Alde Garden;
p.81 courtesy of Jolly Days Luxury Camping;
p.84 courtesy of Hoggarth's Farm Campsite;
p.89 courtesy of 4 Winds Lakeland Tipis;
p.104 courtesy of Acton's Beachside Caravan
& Camping Park; p.106 courtesy of Clachtoll
Beach Campsite

CONTENTS

Introduction 6
How to Build a Campfire 11
Camping at Festivals 15
How to Make Bunting 20
What to Take With You 22

Campsites
  South-West England 25
  South-East England 43
  Central & Eastern England 63
  Northern England 77
  Wales 93
  Scotland & Ireland 99

Camp Cookery
  Recipes 110

INTRODUCTION

My first camping trip was with my best friend in a tiny ridge tent pitched alongside her parents' campervan at Billing Aquadrome. The weekend was full of new experiences: watching the ducks waddle past our tent; eating my first camp-cooked fried breakfast; staying up late with my friend chatting until her dad told us to be quiet; and spending every waking minute in the open air. I had caught the camping bug.

Looking back now I would never choose Billing again, but for a child that hadn't been camping before it was a great introduction. I spent many of the following summers camping with my friend and her parents: travelling around the

UK, visiting places perfect for canoeing and windsurfing or going to campervan meets at racing events. As we got older these trips stopped – until I discovered music festivals. By this time I had all but forgotten how to pitch a tent and what to take with me; how I wish there had been somewhere I could have got advice and guidance. Instead, Reading Festival weekend found me sitting in a leaky tent on a lumpy roll mat with a pot noodle. Since then my love of music and addiction to the festival lifestyle has taken me to hundreds of events all around the country and I have camped at many of them, learning by my mistakes and gathering tips from friends I made along the way.

Keen to prolong that festival feeling I started to explore the idea of visiting campsites but yearned for something a bit different. I wanted to escape the traditional campsite cliché, to avoid campervans and caravans and hordes of people at all costs. I started camping regularly, looking for the ideal campsite, getting back to basics and discovering all that camping in the UK can offer.

Having used nylon tents for years and suffered leaking roofs, condensation in the night and waking to stifling sleeping compartments in the morning, it was a joy to discover canvas again in the form of the bell tent. This is where my addiction to a more considered form of camping came from. I started using campfires to cook on, visiting local farm shops and markets, aspiring to camp in comfort and to share the experience with others. I travelled to a variety of beautiful locations, in all seasons, often with friends who shared the same passion as me.

In our modern lives we spend far too much time rushing around and working far too hard. With the growth of the UK festival scene and camping becoming ever more popular, there are now more camping opportunities than ever: from luxury tented lodges and tipis in National Trust campsites to camping at Loch Ness for Rockness Festival.

This book is an opportunity for you to take advantage of my experience – with useful tips and recommended campsites – and to add your own experiences in the journal sections to share with people you meet or your families in the future. There is nothing like sitting around a campfire with friends, toasting marshmallows, telling stories about your trips. I hope that this book helps you find your perfect pitch and create some amazing memories.

HOW TO BUILD A CAMPFIRE

The best camping memories are often created whilst sitting around a campfire late into the night, sharing ghost stories and listening to music with friends. When all-weather camping it is essential to get a good fire going early, especially if you are looking to cook your meal over it. There are several styles of campfire but the basic 'tipi' structure is described here.

What you need

- A designated fire pit or a dug-out area
- A good-sized pile of dry logs
- Plenty of kindling
- Newspaper, sheets twisted into tapers
- Cotton wool balls
- Firelighters or Mayan dust fire-lighting tinder
- Flint fire steel, matches or lighter

Light your fire

1. Clear the fire pit or dug-out area of any debris.
2. In the centre of the chosen fire area make a small pile out of a mixture of twisted newspaper, kindling and the Mayan dust firelighter tinder or traditional firelighters.
3. Over this pile make a tipi structure with the dry logs, making sure there is space for air to circulate between the logs.
4. Leave a gap at the base so that you can light the tinder/kindling.
5. In between the logs place a couple of cotton wool balls and some twists of newspaper.
6. Build up extra logs behind the fire to create a wall and help dry out the extra logs.
7. Once you are ready, take your fire steel and flint and light the tinder.
8. As the flames take hold add a little more kindling and blow gently to help them spread. If the weather has been dry this can happen surprisingly fast, so be careful.
9. Keep an eye on your fledgling fire, making sure that it doesn't go out. Keep building up the kindling to get a good heat going and once the fire is established add more logs occasionally when needed.

Top tips

- Flint fire steel is the best way of starting a fire (as opposed to matches or lighters) as the chemicals on the fire steel burn at a higher temperature than normal matches or lighters will ever achieve.
- If the weather is bad, place your tinder on duct tape to prevent it from blowing away.
- Building the logs up in a wall behind or around the fire allows them to slowly dry out and also creates a chimney, generating heat rapidly and channelling it towards you.
- Make sure you have access to a bucket of water for fire safety.
- Never leave your fire unattended.

CAMPING AT FESTIVALS

Half the fun of a festival is camping on site. For the cost of the ticket you get yourself a weekend break and can enjoy live performances. After a day watching your favourite bands, there is nothing better than walking with your friends back to your own little pitch and carrying on the fun, sharing stories about the day's adventures. There is a variety of festivals to attend throughout the year but most are now offering weekend camping as an option. Some, like the Green Man Festival in Wales, now offer the opportunity to extend your stay to a week to make the most of the local area. Some festivals are better for camping than others, like The Big Chill Festival or Latitude, and at some, such as Reading and Leeds, you really should be prepared for roughing it. However, just because you are going to a music festival it doesn't mean that you have to live with just the basics, and a little time and planning will make your camping experience a whole lot comfier and happier.

After years of going to festivals across the country and packing for serious glamping trips, as well as having been to festivals with just the bare minimum, I have come up with a few tips.

When you arrive

All festivals now have a car park separate to the camping field, so you will most likely have a long walk with all of your camping gear. Save your arms for lifting pints and all that dancing and invest in a good quality camping trolley. I've seen people using plastic sleighs and rope to drag stuff along but a trolley is worth its weight in gold. If you don't want to fork out for one of your own a few festivals hire out trolleys or wheelbarrows; just be careful of the time as they charge you for going over.

If you are with a group of friends make sure you get a spot large enough for you all. Lay out your camping gear on the floor to reserve space for friends arriving later. Always set up in a circle with a social space at the centre, but don't hog the campsite. Finding the perfect pitch is just a matter of making sure you are not at the bottom of a hill or under a tree in case it rains, close enough but far away enough from the toilets to avoid the smell, and away from the paths so people don't stumble into your tent or wee on it. Don't spend hours dragging your gear around as this is a sure way to make enemies and lose friends. If you are camping alone, try camping near like-minded people; talking on internet forums before you go can help as you may find a loners' camp and make new friends.

Security

By camping in groups or with other people in a similar situation you create your own neighbourhood watch, looking out for each other's belongings. Festivals are known for their lack of security and you will never be able to secure a tent. Do not use a padlock as this is a clear sign to thieves that there are valuables inside. The best advice I can give is to leave valuables at home, split up your cash into a number of pockets or your bag, and sleep with your cash and phone in your sleeping bag.

Finding your tent

When setting up you may want to use a flag to help you spot your tent, and picking a landmark to camp next to always helps. If you are really worried about getting lost make sure you have all of your friends' mobile numbers in your phone. Before you leave for the festival you could even download the Tent Finder App. Don't forget a head torch for those late-night walks back to the tent (and those dreaded trips to the loo) to avoid falling flat on your face over the maze of guy ropes.

What to take

It goes without saying to make sure you've got a decent tent that you can re-use, a sleeping bag, and a self-inflating roll mat. But a few extras can make life a bit easier. Make sure you have anti-bacterial handwash that doesn't need water, plenty of toilet paper, gaffer tape and a mallet. Ear plugs are strongly advised if you plan on snatching any sleep; motorcycle shops sell ones made from soft foam which are more comfortable and more effective than the kind sold at pharmacies. If you are not taking a camping stove and still want a cup of tea or a pot noodle I've found that asking the local burger van for a cup of hot water is an easy solution and saves on the amount you need to carry.

HOW TO MAKE BUNTING

Bunting is beautiful, colourful, retro and fun to make for any special occasion, but is perfect for decorating your tent, awning, campervan, or pitch – why not give your camp the look of the village fete for some vintage glamping? Use your old recycled clothes or any colourful scraps of material, the brighter the better. Bunting is fun to make with the family and can be personalised with lettering or buttons and beads for that extra something special.

What You Need

- Some stiff card
- Scissors
- A coloured pencil or chalk
- A measuring tape
- Selection of fabric cut-offs or recycled clothes
- Pinking sheers
- Sewing machine and thread
- An iron
- Pins
- Ribbon or lace of your choice

How you make it

1. Using the stiff card make a diamond-shaped stencil. If you want bunting with flags of varying size make a couple of differently sized stencils.
2. Take the pinking shears and with the stencil as a guideline cut diamond shapes out of your variety of fabric, making sure you get a good collection of colours and patterns.
3. Fold each diamond in half making a triangle, and assemble into a long line, alternating the different colours and patterns.
4. Measure the desired length of your bunting.
5. Cut the ribbon to the length needed to fit all of your triangles along.
6. Pin the bunting triangles to the ribbon, widest end to the ribbon/lace.
7. Using a sewing machine, stitch the triangles to the ribbon/lace.
8. Once sewn on, iron the bunting flat.

Now your bunting is ready to hang!

WHAT TO TAKE WITH YOU

The list of the equipment that you could take with you is endless. There is such a huge range of kit on offer and if you like your home comforts it can be a chore deciding what to take with you. To make sure you don't overload your car and still forget the essentials amongst your luxuries here is a short list of the basics you should pretty much always take.

- Tent, spare pegs and spare guy ropes
- Good quality sleeping bag
- Air bed or self-inflating roll mat
- Head torch and lantern
- Mallet, with peg extractor
- Toilet roll, wet wipes, anti-bacterial 'no water' handwash
- Lighter, matches or fire steel
- Water carrier
- Gaffer tape
- Waterproofs and wellies
- Sun cream
- Camping chair, waterproof picnic blanket or cushion to sit on
- Camp stove, cooking equipment and spare gas or equipment for cooking on the fire such as Dutch oven, tripod, griddle, grill tray and utensils.

- Kettle
- Washing-up bowl, sponge, eco-friendly washing up liquid and tea-towel
- Crockery
- Cutlery
- Bottle opener
- Tin opener
- Sharp knife
- Spare batteries

Being a camping addict I have my own list of things I won't leave home without. Here is my list of things that make my trips more comfortable:

- Firewood and kindling for the essential campfire (make sure they are allowed on site first)
- Extra woollen blankets and cushions
- Folding Thai cushion for sitting on, or some other form of floor padding such as old sofa cushions.
- Cheap waterproof picnic rugs for extra insulation and to act as carpeting
- Sheepskin rugs
- Wind-up radio
- A good quality canvas tarp so that I can sit out with my friends in all weather
- Good walking shoes for exploring
- Loads of extra layers, gloves and hat for keeping warm
- Solar-powered camp shower
- Coffee percolator
- Camera
- LED frisbee
- Poi
- Pack of playing cards
- Coolbox full of goodies

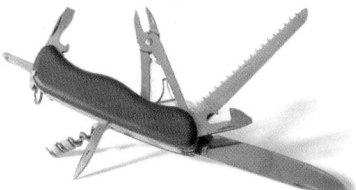

HOLE STATION CAMPSITE
Highampton, Beaworthy, Devon, EX21 5JH
www.holestationcampsite.webs.com

Surrounded by a fairytale forest, Hole Station Campsite is a wonderful secluded pitch in North Devon. The site itself is small and charming, winning you over from the very first moment you arrive to be welcomed by dogs Holly and Star and Mr Crash the goat. Wheelbarrows are on offer for transporting your gear on this car-free site but Greg and his family are more than happy to pitch in if needed. Stargazing from your pitch as you sit around the campfire cannot be beaten; the lack of light pollution in the area makes for a stunning vista. Really good compost toilets and shower facilities, a great location and a relaxed atmosphere make this site a winner. If you lack the necessary equipment, rent-a-tent facilities are available.

⛺ Date: ☁ Weather: 👫 Your Rating: ☆ ☆ ☆ ☆ ☆

⛺ Notes:

DOONE VALLEY CAMPSITE MALMSMEAD
Oaremead Farm, Oare, North Devon, EX35 6NU
www.brendonvalley.co.uk/DooneCampSite.htm

A beautiful isolated campsite located in the centre of Exmoor on the edge of a babbling stream with a small local café selling pizzas within walking distance. Pitches are centred around fire pits to ensure a spacious feeling for the site. Doone Valley camping is as close as you can get to wild camping and still benefit from hot water and showers on hand. Fishing is possible on the river, and there are plenty of walks in the surrounding area so remember your OS map. But if you're not feeling all that energetic, you can simply enjoy the surrounding beauty of sheep-speckled hills and the birds of prey in the sky. The weather on Exmoor can be extreme; make sure you take waterproofs and don't pitch your tent too close to the river in case of a sudden deluge. You should also remember to pack your insect repellent.

Date:　　　　　　　Weather:　　　　　　　Your Rating: ☆ ☆ ☆ ☆ ☆

Notes:

WOODYHYDE CAMPSITE
Valley Road, Isle of Purbeck, Dorset, BH20 5HU
www.woodyhyde.co.uk

Located on Dorset's Jurassic Coast in the heart of Purbeck, Woodyhyde is a large camping ground spread across three fields within 13 acres of land. Purbeck is in the south-eastern corner of the county and is sheltered by amazing coastal scenery. Lulworth, with its dramatic shell-shaped cove, makes the perfect getaway for sun-filled days at the beach, and the Isle of Purbeck itself is renowned for the wildlife that makes its home there. Dolphin spotting, sailing, horse riding and plenty more is on offer nearby. Caravans are not permitted on site and pitches are not marked out so there is space to stretch out in this tent-only ground. Woddyhyde is popular with visitors to the annual 'Chilled Cider' event at the Square & Compass pub in Worth Matravers.

▲ Date: ⛅ Weather: 👫 Your Rating: ☆ ☆ ☆ ☆ ☆

▲ Notes:

YURT CAMP DEVON

Gorse Blossom Farm, Staple Hill Road, Liverton, South Devon, TQ12 6JD
www.yurtcamp.co.uk

Yurt Camp offers a 'glamping' holiday in handmade yurts with central skylights and luxurious furnishings. The traditional yurts offer space and comfort with the added bonus of a wood-burning stove and full-size bed, an easy introduction to camping. Yurt Camp is hidden away in a wooded valley in South Devon, close to Dartmoor and the coast. Launched in 2009 this site offers an ecologically friendly and sustainable alternative to the typical family holiday. With good amenities and plenty of places for the children to explore this makes a great luxurious camping excursion in all weathers for all the family without the hassle of setting up your own tent. This is a complete escape from your normal routine where you can discover the joy of camping.

Date: Weather: Your Rating: ☆ ☆ ☆ ☆ ☆

Notes:

NOONGALLAS
Gulval, Penzance, Cornwall, TR20 8YR
www.kline.freeserve.co.uk

Noongallas Farm is located in the depths of the Cornish countryside. One and a half miles from the nearest village and two miles from Penzance, this pitch is not exactly convenient for local amenities but once you have your supplies there is little reason to leave such a perfect location. The barn is a central point in bad weather, providing refuge and occasional open-mic nights, the sense of community winning over campers time and again. Fairytale woodland surrounds Noongallas and feels truly magical; it's great for the kids to explore, with its bubbling river, waterfalls and rope swings. Campfires and BBQs are permitted and the owners, John and Kay, love to encourage acoustic music round the campfire and local bands sometimes perfom in the barn.

▲ Date: ⛅ Weather: 👫 Your Rating: ☆ ☆ ☆ ☆ ☆

▲ Notes:

NAMPARRA CAMPSITE
Kugar, Nr Helston, Cornwall, TR12 7LY
www.namparracampsite.co.uk

Ten minutes' walk from the beautiful Blue Flag beach of Kennack Sands is Namparra Campsite, 6 acres of meadow with stunning sea views. Near to charming Helston on the Lizard Peninsula, this simple rural campsite is a fabulous location. Family-run with good basic facilities and a log cabin shop for any essentials you may have forgotten, as well as fresh bread and butter. Potters Bar, the local pub, is within walking distance and has live music, local cider and even takeaway pizza. Cagdwith is a short drive away with its pub, fishing competitions and summer fish BBQs. Once on site you may want to take a walk around and explore, feed the ducks on the pond and say hello to the resident pygmy goats Toggles and Cinnamon. A friendly, traditional Cornish campsite.

Date: Weather: Your Rating: ☆ ☆ ☆ ☆ ☆

Notes:

THISTLEDOWN CENTRE
Tinkley Lane, Nympsfield, Stroud, Gloucestershire, GL10 3HU
www.thistledown.org.uk

Thistledown is an environmentally friendly, family-run camping and education centre focusing on the relationship between land and life. Set in the Cotswold Area of Outstanding Natural Beauty just above the small town of Nailsworth, Thistledown is spread across natural glades in historic woodland and meadows, with rambling paths, streams and ponds, and the occasional piece of artwork hidden amongst picnic spots and camping glades in elderflower orchards. This camping ground is about discovering your own space, watching the wildlife and enjoying the night sky as you sit round your campfire, and hopefully learning from the experience. With compost toilets and solar shower tents you can truly revel in the green camping ethos.

▲ Date: ⛅ Weather: 👥 Your Rating: ☆ ☆ ☆ ☆ ☆

▲ Notes:

SUMMER MEADOWS

The Hide Out, Forda, Croyde, North Devon, EX33 1JG
www.summermeadows.co.uk

This is a small independent campsite in the surfer's haven of Croyde, a traditional village with a trendy atmosphere on the north coast of Devon. Croyde is one of my favourite destinations throughout the year, especially when the school holidays are over, leaving the campsites and roads emptier. Summer Meadows is close to numerous sandy beaches, a short distance from Exmoor and surrounded by fantastic countryside. It provides campers with a welcome alternative to the larger sites taking over Croyde. Facilities are adequate, with a tiki-style shower hut, communual BBQ and wetsuit drying area. It is ecologically friendly with recycling and compost points as well as chickens and ducks for free-range eggs. This site makes an ideal base from which explore the surrounding area.

Date: Weather: Your Rating: ☆ ☆ ☆ ☆ ☆

Notes:

WESTERMILL FARM HOLIDAYS
Exford, Nr Minehead, Somerset, TA24 7NJ
www.westermill.com

This is a lovely quiet campsite, disturbed only by the sounds of the resident cattle. Beautiful pitches are set in four fields in a secluded valley bordered by the River Exe in the centre of Exmoor. Relax as your children play in the river, bathe in the cool waters yourself or try your hand at fishing. Westermill is a laid-back site for campers looking to get back to basics and explore the delights of Devon. This really is a child's paradise where you can let the little ones wander off while you kick back with a glass of wine and chat to the other campers. It is recommended you avoid camping right by the river in case of flooding and to avoid midges. However, an all-round great campsite with good facilities, allowing campfires in one of the fields, and with a well-stocked shop selling a variety of its own free-range products.

▲ Date: Weather: Your Rating: ☆ ☆ ☆ ☆ ☆

▲ Notes:

BRYHER CAMPSITE
Bryher, Isles of Scilly, TR23 0PR
www.bryhercampsite.co.uk

'A totally natural campsite for the true camper' protected in a natural valley and sitting on the breathtaking island of Bryher in the Scilly Isles. The pitches here are becoming ever more popular and booking a spot in advance is advisable. As far as you can get from campsites with club houses and swimming pools, Bryher is a more rugged camping experience, but due to its location people with physical disabilities may find it a difficult proposition. The Scilly Isles are made up of five small islands so why not explore the rest by boat, take an evening trip or go seal spotting for the day? Bryher is a wonderful rugged little island with hidden coves, rocky granite outcrops and tons of wildlife to keep an eye out for. Travel to the site is by boat from St Mary's Island so make sure you take only what you can carry.

Date: Weather: Your Rating: ☆ ☆ ☆ ☆ ☆

Notes:

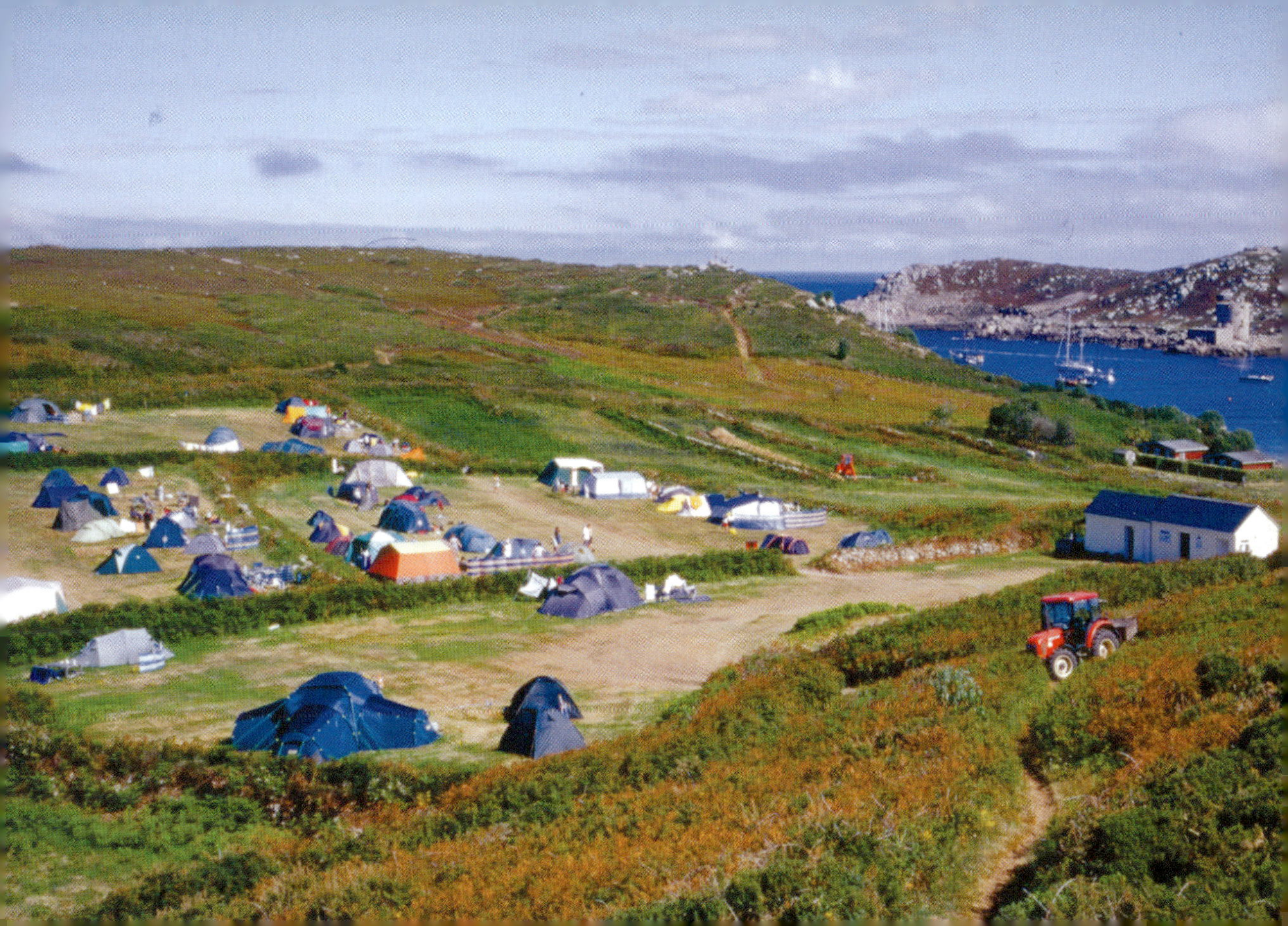

LITTLE WENFORK
Rezare, Launceston, Cornwall, PL15 9NU
www.littlewenfork.co.uk

A welcoming and tiny campsite that allows a maximum of only five pitches; with just the sound of animals and your fellow campers surrounding you this makes a perfect escape. Based on gently sloping grass plots surrounded by open fields and unobstructed views to Bodmin Moor and Dartmoor, you feel as if you are having the pleasure of camping in the most perfect private garden. Within easy access to the beaches of the north and south coasts as well as the rolling countryside of west Devon, this is a great campsite from which to explore the contrasting landscape of the West Country. The Springer Spaniel pub is only half a mile away down a country track and serves real ale and good food made from locally sourced produce.

▲ Date:	⛅ Weather:	👫 Your Rating: ☆ ☆ ☆ ☆ ☆

▲ Notes:

BOTREA TIPIS AND YURTS
West Penwith, Cornwall
www.botrea.co.uk

A lovely Cornish holiday spot and a green and organic experience to boot, Botrea is a working farm with both Mongolian yurts and North American tipis available to hire. Botrea prides itself on being the only organic farm in Cornwall in an Area of Oustanding Natural Beauty. West Penwith is the southernmost area of England and is full of dramatic beaches, wooded valleys, moorland and hidden coves. The sea in this area is often crystal clear and jade green while the Land's End peninsula, rarely suffering from cold weather, makes a great location for outdoor activities. Courses such as bushcraft, willow weaving, bow making and yurt construction are on offer, but if you are looking for something a little more romantic or want to bring along the grandparents, why not book up the newly converted tractor shed?

Date:　　　　　Weather:　　　　　Your Rating: ☆ ☆ ☆ ☆ ☆

Notes:

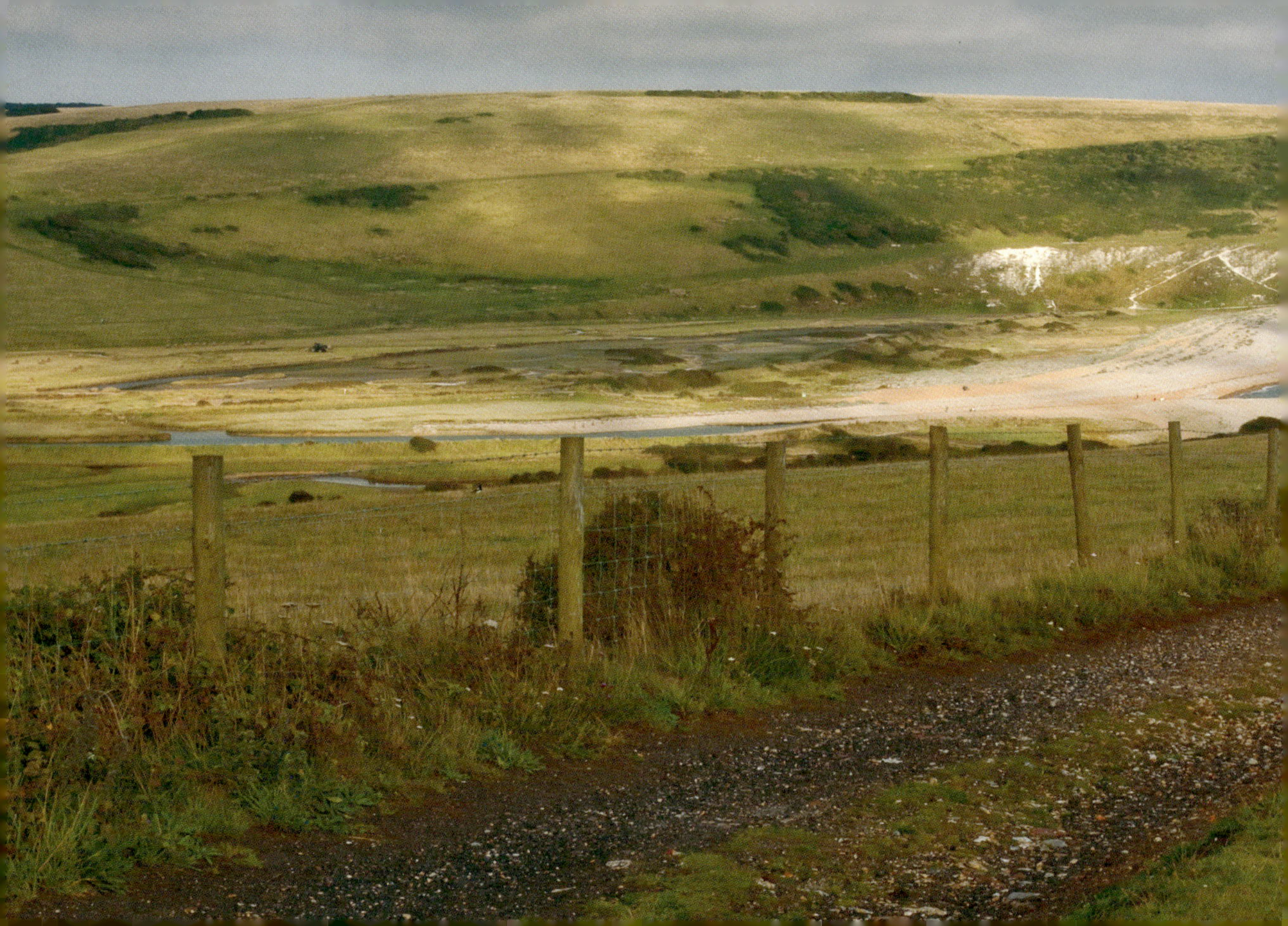

SOUTH-EAST ENGLAND

WELSUMMER
Chalk House, Lenham Road, Harrietsham, Kent, ME17 1 NQ
www.welsummer.moonfruit.co.uk

This is a wonderful little site with a truly relaxed atmosphere. Personal touches from owners Med and Laura make it a very special place to camp. Pancakes, fresh eggs, herbs, muffins, coffee and ice creams are all on offer at the site office, and attention paid to such small details guarantees campers a unique experience. You can have the choice of a field or a woodland pitch and all have a designated firepit. The showers are heated by a wood-burning stove and the facilities are basic but this adds to the rustic charm of this site. The woodland has special memories for Laura's family and so great care is taken to make sure that it is nurtured. Woodland walks lead to the Pepper Box Inn, a great place for a pint of Kentish ale and a ploughman's before your walk back to light the campfire.

▲ Date: Weather: Your Rating: ☆ ☆ ☆ ☆ ☆

▲ Notes:

EVERGREEN FARM WOODLAND CAMPSITE
West Hoathly Road, East Grinstead, West Sussex, RH19 4NE

Only an hour's drive away from London and close enough to the M25 to make this an easy commute. This really is back to basics camping with very few facilities but a great taste of what outdoor life should really be like. If you need your home comforts this is not the place for you. There is a portaloo on site but water is delivered in containers, along with the wood for your fire. Just being here makes you feel a part of the farming lifestyle, with horses, sheep, dogs and pigs for company, giving you a taste of the Sussex countryside. The pitches are set in small clearings amongst 10 acres of idyllic woodland teeming with wildlife. Two types of pitches are available, some more secluded than others. Pack light as there is no parking next to your pitch and quad bikes with trailers are used to transport your equipment.

Date:　　　　　Weather:　　　　　Your Rating: ☆ ☆ ☆ ☆ ☆

Notes:

ROSEMARY VINEYARD
Smallbrook Lane, Ryde, Isle of Wight, PO33 4BE
www.rosemaryvineyard.co.uk

A unique campsite set in a large vineyard. Make the most of the milder Isle of Wight climate: make camp in the estate overlooking the vines, relax and enjoy the good life. Stroll around the site enjoying the views and purchase some wine or cider from the shop to drink whilst taking in the peace of the surroundings. With only twelve pitches this is a relatively small and exclusive camping ground. Take advantage of the free admission to the vineyard for tastings and tours and pick up your complimentary bottle of wine from the vineyard for your pitch booking. The shop on site sells all sorts of local produce from mustards to sweets from the Needles Factory. The park is located in a 30-acre estate in the middle of the Isle of Wight countryside but still within walking distance of Ryde and the local beaches.

Date: **Weather:**   **Your Rating:** ☆ ☆ ☆ ☆ ☆

Notes:

HURST VIEW (SOLENT VIEW) CAMPING
Lower Pennington Lane, Lymington, Hampshire, SO41 8AL
www.hurstviewleisure.co.uk

A peaceful and sedate site that allows campfires, Hurst View is located on the edge of the New Forest National Park in Hampshire. With good (if aged) basic facilities and a sea view, this site makes a welcome change from the traditional, high-desnsity New Forest pitches. Lymington, the closest village, is just a short drive away. This is a great real camping site, with ample space for you to spread out, a nature reserve at the end of the park, and a wonderful walk down to the sea for early-morning swims. The site itself is spread over three large fields and there is no limit to the number of pitches that can be set, so if you are looking for a relaxed bank holiday getaway at the last minute then this site is always worth a shot.

▲ Date: Weather: Your Rating: ☆ ☆ ☆ ☆ ☆

▲ Notes:

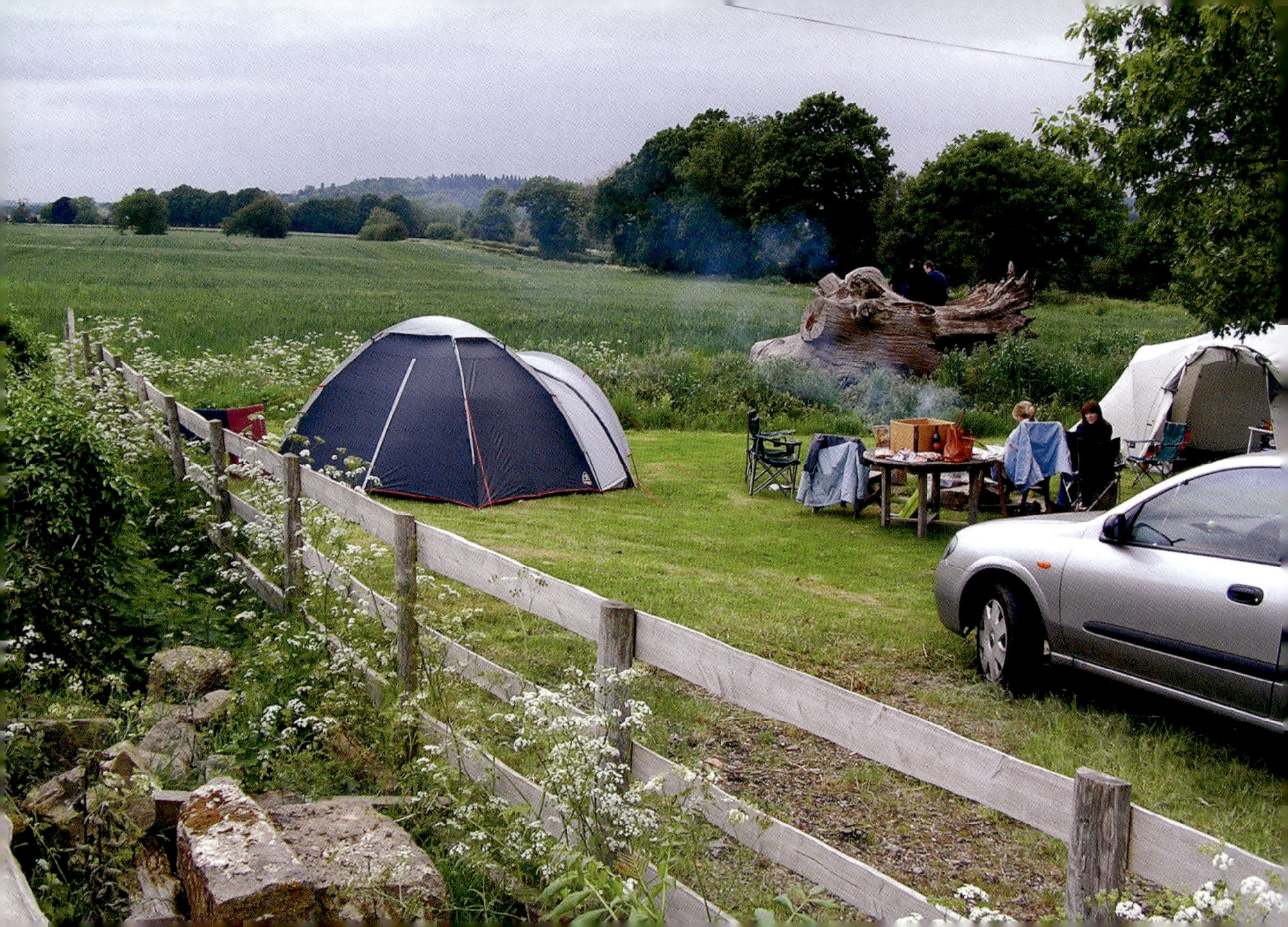

MANOR COURT FARM
Ashurst, Tunbridge Wells, Kent, TN3 9TB
www.manorcourtfam.co.uk

Manor Court Farm is a bed and breakfast farmhouse with both a camping field and a more informal garden camping area. The farm is a collection of traditional Kentish buildings with 350 acres of working farmland; children will love the chickens roaming the fields as well as the rabbits and guinea pigs in the petting area. This park is set in the heart of the Garden of England and really is like something out of *The Darling Buds of May*; you can buy fresh milk from the farmhouse whilst you let the children explore amongst the fruit trees and rope swings. There are good clean facilities on site, and each pitch has its own designated fire pit, with garden furniture or tree stumps for seating. Just a short drive from Tunbridge Wells but far enough away to feel like a real rural retreat, this is a great location for a family break.

Date: Weather: Your Rating: ☆ ☆ ☆ ☆ ☆

Notes:

RED SHOOT CAMPING PARK
Linwood, Ringwood, Hampshire, BH24 3QT
www.redshoot-campingpark.com

In the heart of the New Forest the pitches here are next door to a pub, the Red Shoot Inn, which serves a good variety of home-cooked food and even has a microbrewery on site. Why not plan your trip to coincide with one of the beer festivals, and pitch your tent within staggering distance? This part of the New Forest is one of the most attractive and unspoilt areas with fantastic walks, forest ponies, quaint little villages, streams and babbling brooks all in close proximity. The campsite itself has very good facilities, with plenty of showers and toilets, a well-stocked shop and a laundry room. Be careful with your choice of pitch as there are a few towards the far end of the site that are prone to flooding in bad weather. All together a good family campsite but one that can get extremely busy over bank holiday weekends.

Date:　　　　　　　Weather:　　　　　　　Your Rating: ☆ ☆ ☆ ☆ ☆

Notes:

ROEBECK CAMPING & CARAVAN PARK

Gatehouse Road, Ryde, Isle Of Wight, PO33 4BP
www.roebeck-farm.co.uk www.tipiholidays.co.uk

Roebeck Farm offers good pitching ground on the edge of the seaside resort of Ryde and is a perfect base from which to explore the Solent side of the island. A small friendly site with good basic facilities, it is conveniently located close to the local shops and beaches. Roebeck is a great way to introduce the family to proper camping, with campfires glowing at night, rabbits hopping through the fields, ducks and geese waddling around the site, and an introductory taste of the Isle of Wight. For those without their own tents, or who fancy something a little different, Sioux Tipis are available to hire and overlook an attractive fishing lake.

Date: Weather: Your Rating: ☆ ☆ ☆ ☆ ☆

Notes:

HIDDEN SPRING VINEYARD

Vines Cross Road, Horham, East Sussex, TN21 OHG
www.hiddenspring.co.uk

Set on a smallholding and a real labour of love for the owners, this site is small and select with a variety of pitches available. Whilst part of the land is reserved for caravan plots, tent pitches are in an adjacent field and all have designated fire rings. There are also two yurts available to hire which come with all the basic equipment; if you fancy something a little different a geo-dome or bell tent can also be rented on request. Sample some of the site's organic cider or apple juice and keep an eye out for the abundant local wildlife; you may even spot a badger or two mooching past your tent. A local shop, a pub and a café are all within walking distance.

Date: Weather: Your Rating: ☆ ☆ ☆ ☆ ☆

Notes:

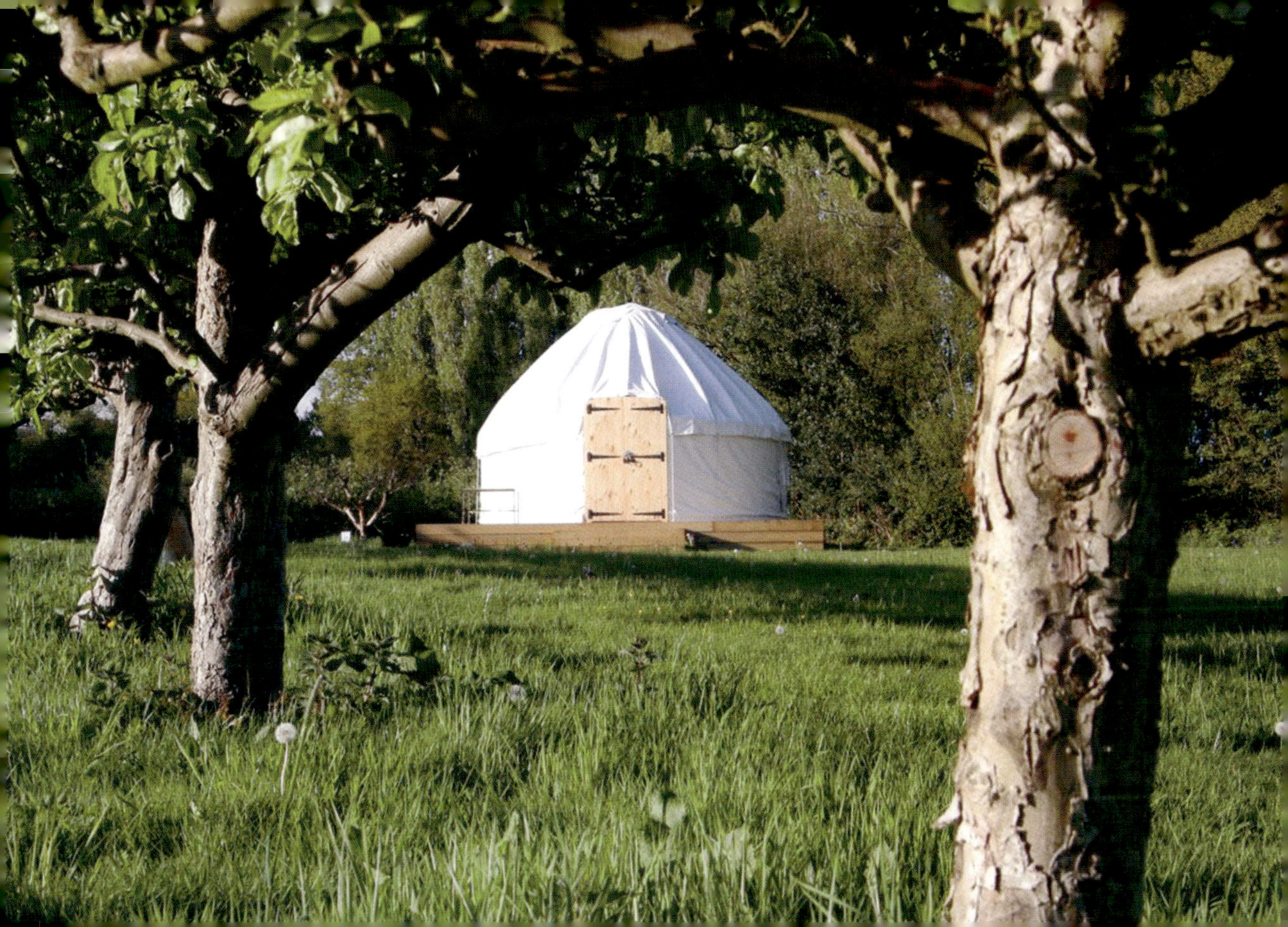

BILLY CAN CAMPING
Manor farm, Arundel, West Sussex, BN18 OBG
www.billycancamping.co.uk

Billy Can offers luxury camping in pre-pitched bell tents with all the necessities provided for you, not to mention the many extra glamorous touches. Just bring your sleeping bag and your own provisions and make the most of this back-to-nature stay-cation. A retro camping experience on a working farm, your experience here can be as communal or as individual as you desire. A mess tent provides all the extras you may need and eco toilet and showers add a rustic edge to the whole experience. Billy Can is walking distance from historic Arundel and its castle, and, perched as it is next to the river Arun, makes for a beautiful little sustainable site in the South Downs.

▲ Date: ⛅ Weather: 👫 Your Rating: ☆ ☆ ☆ ☆ ☆

▲ Notes:

HOOK FARM CAMPSITE
Hook Lane, West Hoathy, West Sussex, RH19 4PT
www.hook-farm.co.uk

Sister site to Kitts Cottage Camp, Hook Farm is another stunning small campsite. Located on elevated ground with panoramic views over ancient woodland to the South Downs, it is within easy walking distance of the village of West Hoathly and its popular pub. The number of pitches is limited and, with only basic facilities available, this site will not appeal to all. But if you are looking for a tranquil back-to-basics experience then Hook Farm will tick all your boxes. The owners aim to maintain the natural beauty of the area and provide a real camping experience focused on a pure environment and the tranquil pleasure of a good fire. What more could you ask for?

Date:	Weather:	Your Rating: ☆ ☆ ☆ ☆ ☆

Notes:

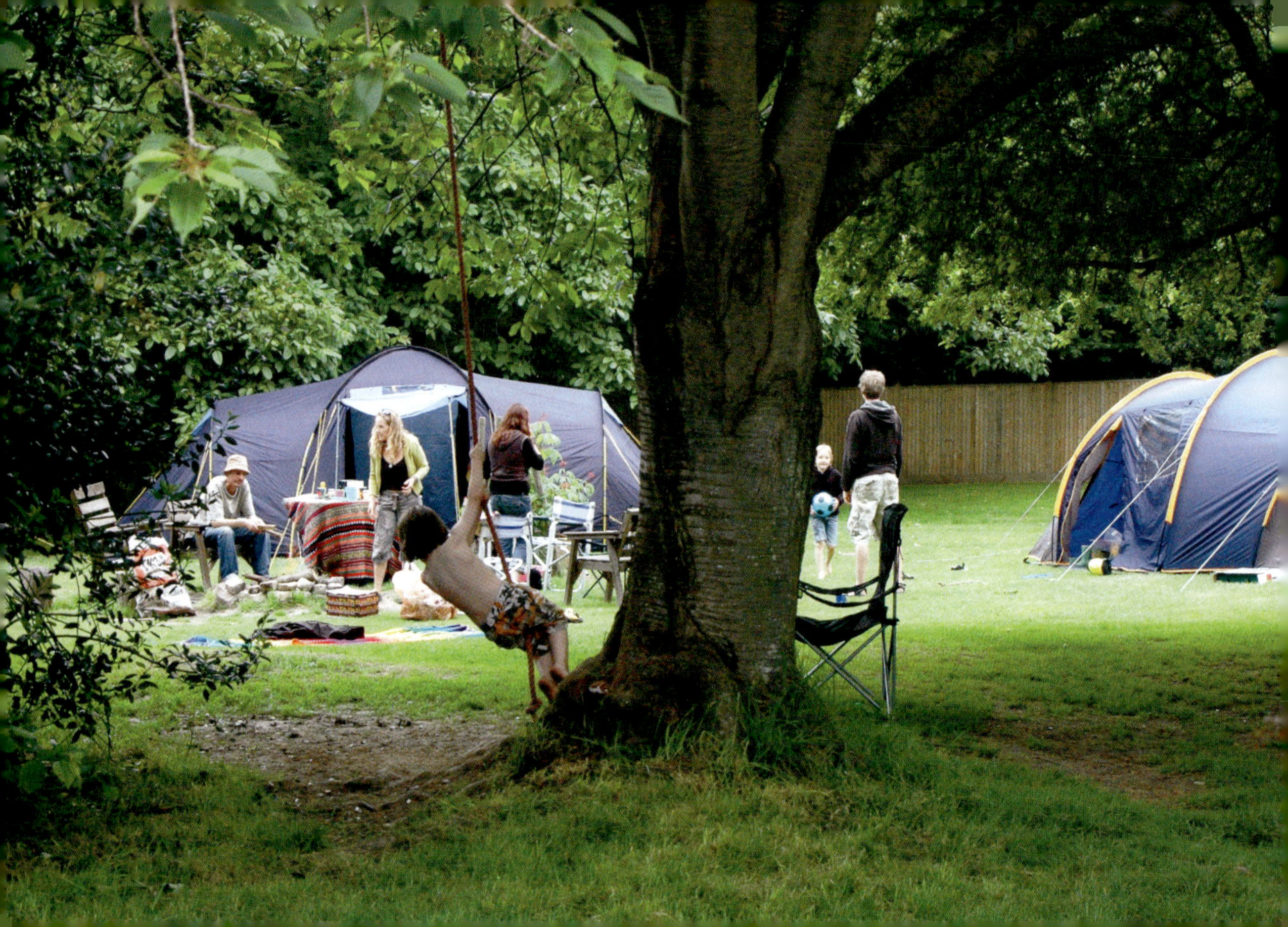

CROFT COTTAGE CAMPING

Croft Cottage, Godhill, Fordingbridge, Hampshire, SP6 2LE
www.croftcottagenewforest.co.uk

Croft Cottage is a little jewel: an idyllic, peaceful cottage campsite with 2 acres of gardens, a paddock and a camping field. Fifteen marked pitches are located around the edge of the camping field on freshly mown grass, with a badminton and volleyball net in the centre. The camp has the feel of a traditional camping site from days gone by with a more personal touch in comparison to its neighbour, the larger and more commercial Sandy Balls Holiday Centre. Kids are free to explore, collecting eggs from the chickens in the morning, visiting the horses in the paddock and climbing to the treehouse. The beauty of the New Forest is right on your doorstep and popular tourist towns, including Bournemouth, are only a short drive away.

Date: Weather: Your Rating: ☆ ☆ ☆ ☆ ☆

Notes:

KITTS COTTAGE CAMPSITE
Freshfield Place Farm, Slop Lane, Scaynes Hill, West Sussex, RH17 7NP
www.kittscamp.co.uk

Located between Lewes and Haywards Heath, Kitts Camp is a treasure in the centre of the lush Sussex countryside. Pitches are in a relaxed, secluded glade on the edge of sheltered woodland. Close to a myriad of public footpaths and with very basic facilities, Kitts is a perfect for a romantic retreat or for larger groups as there is enough space to escape to your own little corner. James, the owner, maintains a site where campfires are encouraged and is keen not to overfill the camp ground. You can see the Bluebell Railway as you arrive at Kitts Camp, so it is within easy walking distance. Also within walking distance is the Sloop Inn, a great little pub for real ale and good country cooking. Ashdown Forest, the home of Winnie the Pooh, is right on your doorstep along with other places to visit such as Heaver and Leeds castles.

▲ Date:　　　　　　　　☁ Weather:　　　　　　　　👫 Your Rating: ☆ ☆ ☆ ☆ ☆

▲ Notes:

PALACE FARM CAMP SITE
Down Court road, Doddington, Sittingbourne, Kent, ME9 0AU
www.palacefarm.com

'If you are looking to party', warns the website, 'this is not the site for you'. This is a small, family run campsite with just twenty-five pitches located in Doddinton. It offers a perfect escape and is near a sleepy little village, with a butcher, a garage with convenience store and a great local pub, the Chequers, serving the most amazing roast lunch. The pitches here are huge, and are laid out around the edges of the fields to emphasise the feeling of individual seclusion. Hiring a fire pit is well worth it, especially to cook your steak from the butcher over the flames. Based on working farmland and surrounded by orchards, this is a delightful place to pitch up.

▲ Date: ☼ Weather: ♚ Your Rating: ☆ ☆ ☆ ☆ ☆

▲ Notes:

FORGE WOOD CAMPING
Sham Farm Road, Eridge Green, Tunbridge Wells, Kent, TN3 9JD
www.forgewoodcamping.co.uk

Forge Wood offers freedom for your children to explore acres of ancient woodland in which they can hunt for Iron Age forts, Victorian follies and deer skulls and build hidden dens. This site is set on the Eridge Park Estate, one of the country's largest deer parks. A real wilderness woodland location, albeit one with good modern toilet and shower facilities, Forge Wood is a great site for introducing children to proper camping, and a great natural playground where they can climb trees, play on rope swings, collect wood for the fire, or simply watch the wildlife. Electronic music is not allowed on site but acoustic music is welcomed.

▲ Date: Weather: Your Rating: ☆ ☆ ☆ ☆ ☆

▲ Notes:

UPPER MORGAY WOOD
Cripps Corner, Staplewood, Hastings, East Sussex, TN32 5SH

The only entertainment at this site is the menagerie of farm animals: donkeys, geese, hens and dogs! This is a small and welcoming field-based camping ground, surrounded by woodland and meadows. Rambling woodland walks lead from the campsite to a delightful local pub that specialises in 12-hour roasted pig and honeycomb ice cream, a welcome treat after the walk there. Fires are allowed in designated fire pits and wood can be purchased on site. If you want to pitch in a field and be left to your own devices, Upper Morgay should suit you down to the ground.

▲ Date: Weather: Your Rating: ☆ ☆ ☆ ☆ ☆

▲ Notes:

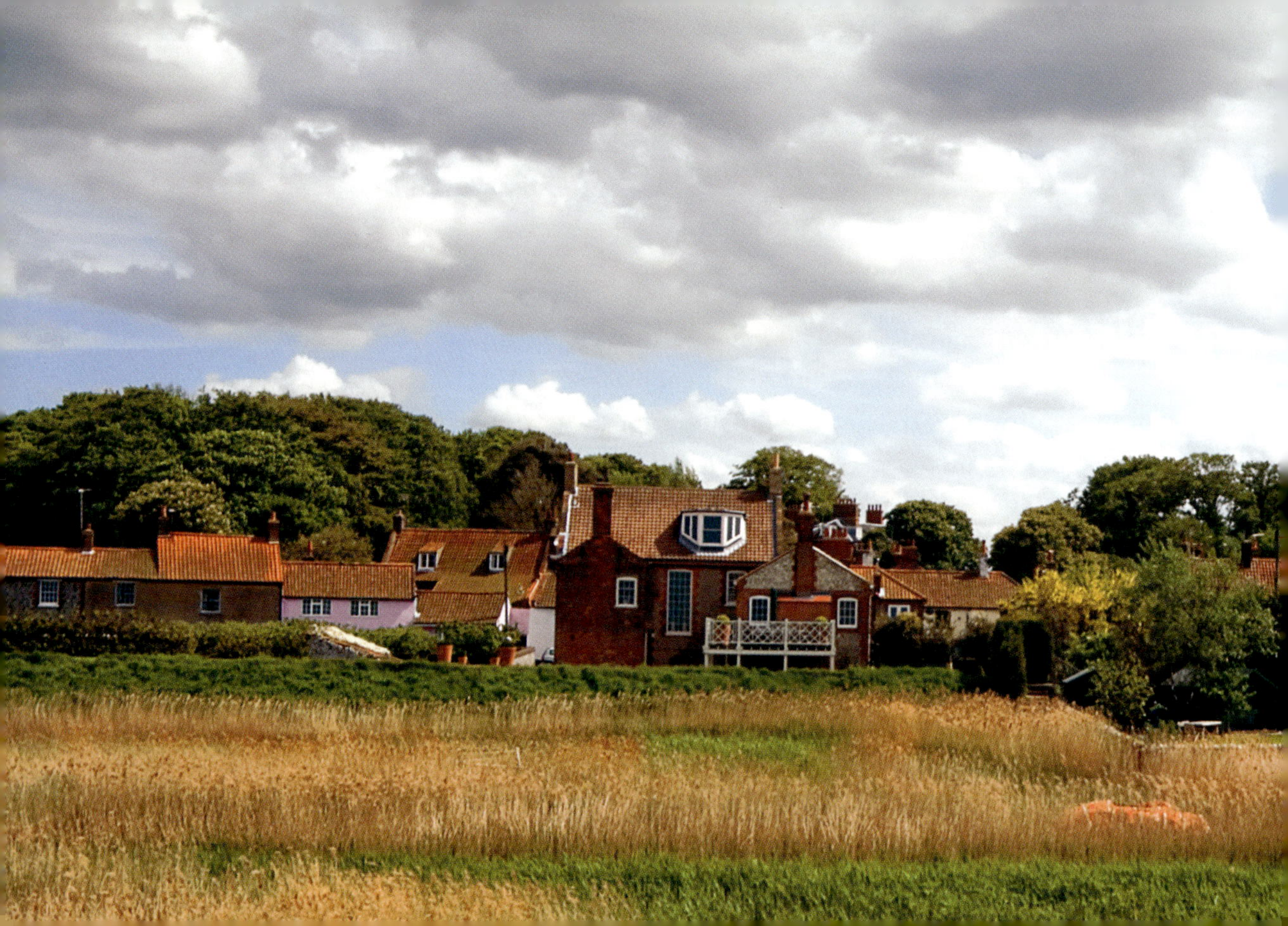

CENTRAL & EASTERN ENGLAND

YELLOW WOOD BUSH CAMPS
Bush Camps, Hay-on-Wye, Herefordshire
www.bushcraftadventures.com

A peaceful woodland retreat of a camp with a real emphasis on getting back to nature, this isn't just a course location but a real earthy camp ground with open fires and like-minded campers. Not only are weekend bushcraft courses available on this site but a variety of afternoon courses are on offer too, covering everything from outdoor living (including wild cookery) to wilderness survival, fire-making and tree-climbing: perfect for families and for smaller groups genuinely interested in making the most of this idyllic environment. Dogs are not allowed, and the owners gently suggest that campers avoid bringing 'huge family dome tents'. Be warned that the 'basic' lavatories may not be to everyone's satisfaction!

Date: Weather: Your Rating: ☆ ☆ ☆ ☆ ☆

Notes:

AZURE SEAS HOLIDAY VILLAGE
The Street, Corton, Nr Lowestoft, Suffolk
www.azureseas.co.uk

A tranquil park kept natural and quiet to prevent the traditional holiday village feel, Azure Seas is a caravan site with space dedicated to tents and tourers. I don't normally like to recommend locations that are dominated by caravans but this pitch has the benefit of being set on a clifftop overlooking the Suffolk coast. The pitches are within woodland and some give a stunning view of the setting sun. There is also a quiet little pub located next to the site and Corton is a short walk away. If that's not enough to justify its popularity, Azure Seas has its own private beach for peaceful days of basking in the sun and bathing in summer. If you are attending Latitude Festival and are looking for somewhere to stay to extend your trip, Azure Seas would be a perfect pit stop.

▲ Date:　　　　　　　Weather:　　　　　　　Your Rating: ☆ ☆ ☆ ☆ ☆

▲ Notes:

BIG SKY RETREAT
Old Station, Station Road, Haddiscoe, NR31 9JA
www.bigskyretreat.co.uk

Offering quirky camping in massive army surplus tents on the edge of the Broadland National Park, this is a luxury site in a half-acre estate under the wide open skies of the Norfolk Broads. Big Sky offers a unique and exclusive camping experience in military-style lodge tents, with toilet and shower facilities in a converted Second World War pillbox. With grassland to wade through on sunny days, a willow tree to climb, and a large fire pit for cooking marshmallows, Big Sky Retreat retains the basic elements of traditional camping but has the added glamour of your very own pre-pitched tent containing all that you may need: proper beds, rustic furniture, rugs and throws. If you are planning a romantic retreat then champagne and flowers can be booked for your arrival.

▲ Date: ❄ Weather: ♥♥ Your Rating: ☆ ☆ ☆ ☆ ☆

▲ Notes:

BRECK FARM
Weybourne, Holt, Norfolk, NR25 6QL
www.beckfarm.co.uk

A family-owned farm campsite in the North Norfolk countryside close to the cosmopolitan town of Holt and the beaches of Weybourne. The owners of Breck Farm pride themselves on having run the farm and adjoining campsite for over 50 years, and on the fact that regulars keep coming back time and time again. Field-based pitches with no marked-out plots give this site the higgledy-piggledy feel of festival camping at times but the owners are careful never to over-book the space and there is always room to be found within this little piece of Norfolk. The farm shop on-site is well worth a visit for the Norfolk pink potatoes and for fresh free-range eggs. An easy-going site allowing open campfires and good, if basic, facilities.

Date: Weather: Your Rating: ☆ ☆ ☆ ☆ ☆

Notes:

Bishop's Castle

FOXHOLES CASTLE CAMPING
Montgomery Road, Shropshire, SY9 5HA
www.foxholes-castle.co.uk

Foxholes Camping is a good family location in south-west Shropshire's beautiful hill country. Bishop's Castle is walking distance from the campsite via the Shropshire Way footpath, through open fields and past luscious panoramic views. If you are a real ale fan there are a couple of brewery pubs that you should make a pit stop at, The Three Tuns being the pick of them. The village has numerous events throughout the year that attract visitors including beer and walking festivals. The pitches themselves are exposed to the elements so make sure you have good quality tent pegs and make the most of the stunning scenery surrounding the camp ground. Fires are allowed as long as you use a raised fire pit and the grass is not scorched; make sure you take your own wood as it is not available on site.

Date:	Weather:	Your Rating: ☆ ☆ ☆ ☆ ☆

Notes:

THE COATES FARM
Rushbury, Church Stretton, Shropshire, SY6 7DZ

A tiny and friendly camping field with a relaxed atmosphere on a working farm, Coates Farm is a small site big on helping its guests get back to nature. With only five pitches, this site offers all comers a great opportunity to kick back far away from the holiday season hordes. Facilities are understandably basic, but if you are a tennis fan there is a court available to use, and with three good pubs all within walking distance this campsite is an ideal base of operations for real ale drinkers on a weekend away. Well-behaved pets are allowed on site, and with walking routes such as Wenlock Edge nearby to help you tire out your pooch, this is also a great campsite for dog owners.

Date: Weather: Your Rating: ☆ ☆ ☆ ☆ ☆

Notes:

TRESSECK CAMP SITE
Hoarwithy, Hereford, Herefordshire, HR2 6QJ
www.tresseckcampsite.co.uk

Tresseck is a very basic campsite in Hoarwithy village, down a dirt track next to the New Harp Inn, and set on the banks of the River Wye. Whilst the river can have a very strong current and is fenced off so that children do not have direct access, fishing is encouraged from the river and this spot would be perfect for anglers. Set in a meadow and catering for tents only, there is space for you to stretch out and enjoy the peace of this Herefordshire village. The river also has a natural landing site and so is perfect for watersports or just paddling with your kids. The emphasis here is on a peaceful, family experience; loud music and alcohol are forbidden, although there is a good pub two minutes' walk away.

Date: Weather: Your Rating: ☆ ☆ ☆ ☆ ☆

Notes:

ALDE GARDEN

The White Horse Inn, Low Road, Sweffling, Suffolk, IP17 2BB
www.aldegarden.co.uk

In the heart of Suffolk, with its wide open spaces and beautiful coastline, Alde Garden is a perfect setting for a low-impact holiday with an added touch of luxury. There are basic tent pitches available or, if you fancy something a little special, there are Mongolian yurts, Native American tipis, a traditional carved Gypsy caravan and even a secret 'Romantic Hideout'. The Hideout is a wooden, tent-shaped structure on stilts, with a clear roof for star gazing, and is located in a small clearing. The site itself is located in the Alde Valley and is surrounded by stunning countryside and farmland. Numerous farm shops and pubs are within driving distance and make for a perfect gourmet stay-cation. Well worth a visit is Framlingham with its castle, and the nearby Shawsgate Vineyard for local wine.

▲ Date: ☼ Weather: 👬 Your Rating: ☆ ☆ ☆ ☆ ☆

▲ Notes:

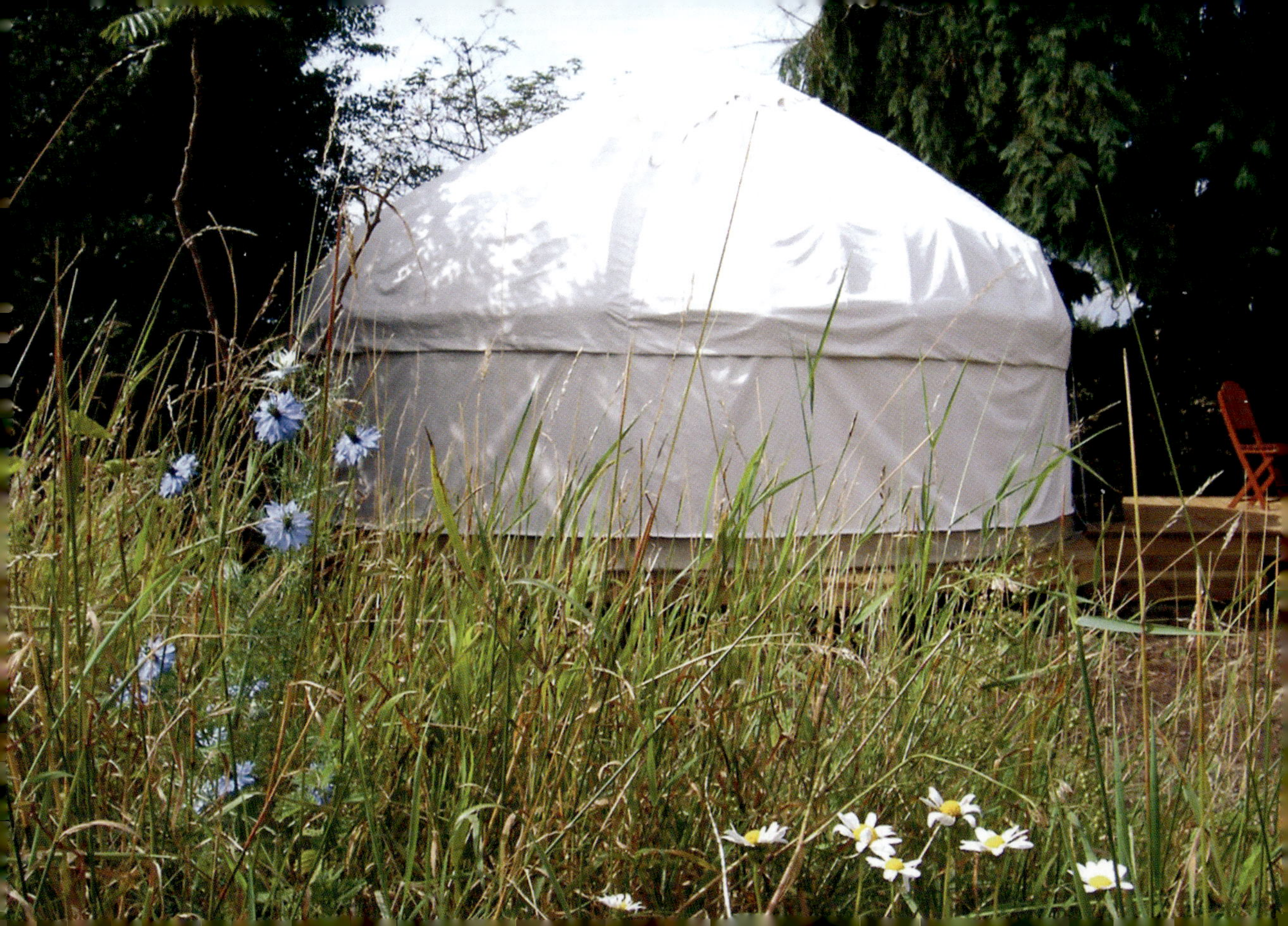

HOPLEYS CAMPING & CARAVAN SITE
Doddingtree Farm, Cleobury Road, Bewdley, Worcestershire, DY12 2QL
www.hopleyscamping.co.uk

Attractive surroundings in which to pitch your tent, nestled in the Severn Valley close to the town of Bewdley and the ancient woodland of the Wyre Forest. Hopleys is known as a tranquil site from which to explore the West Midlands, and with a fishing pool, farm shop and deli, and seasonal fruit picking, this pitch could be a real charmer. All manner of campers are welcome to this relaxed site with views of the surrounding farmland. If you don't fancy cooking on your BBQ or camp fire, take a trip to Bewdley for some highly recommended fish and chips from the Merchant Fish Bar, or try the on-site café.

Date: Weather: Your Rating: ☆ ☆ ☆ ☆ ☆

Notes:

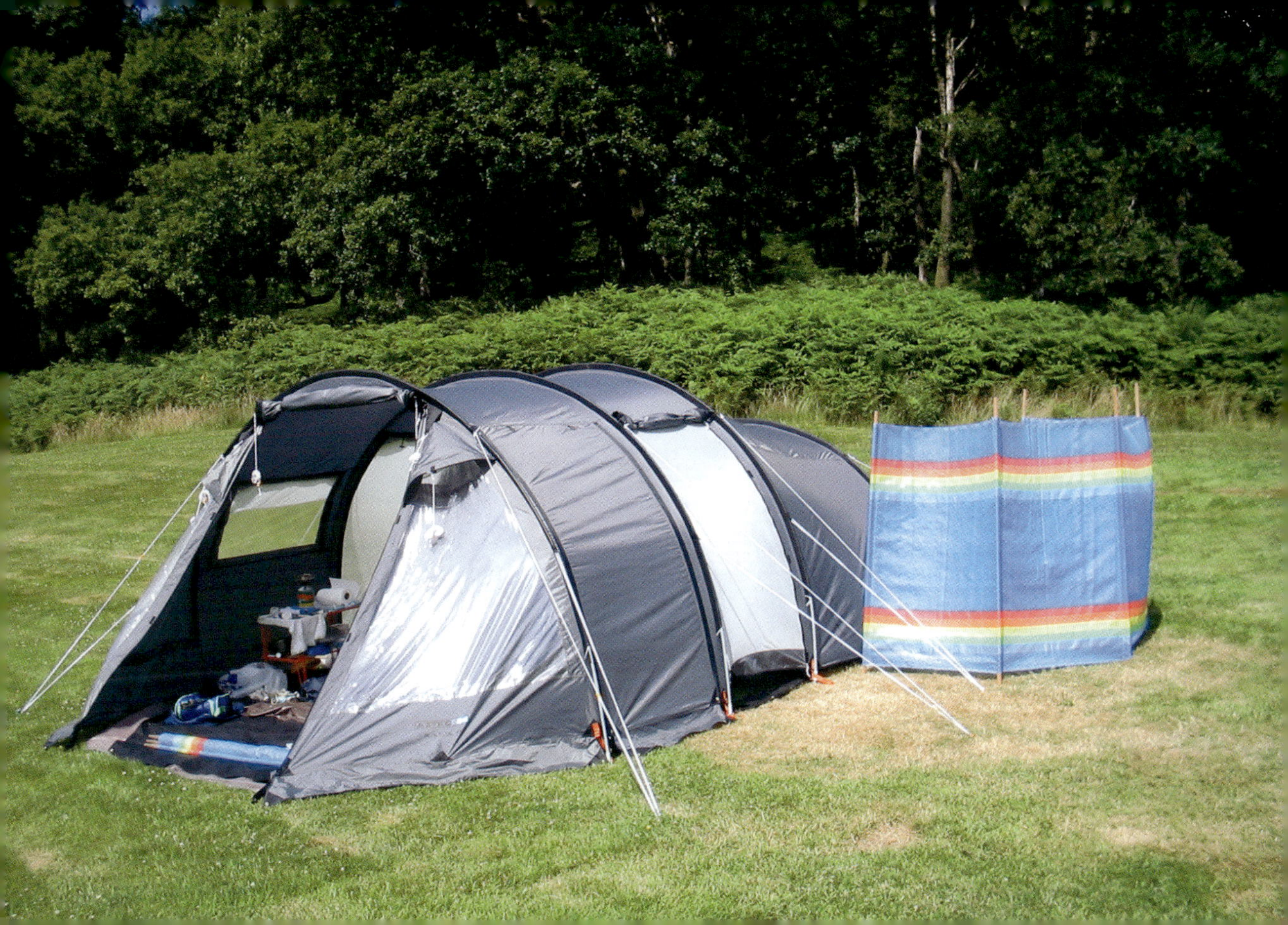

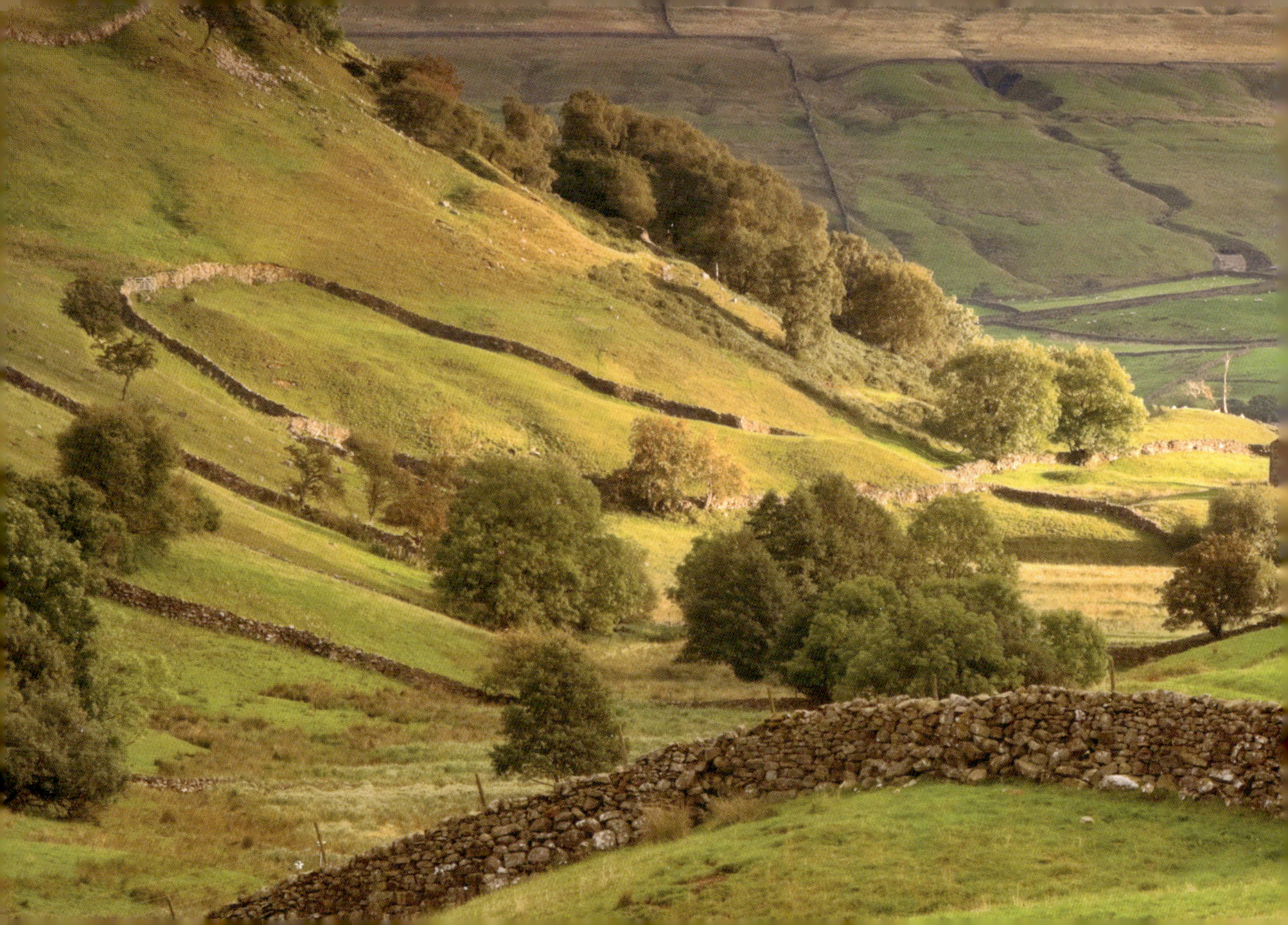

NORTHERN ENGLAND

BOBBYBEE'S CARAVAN SITE/MERE FARM CAMP SITE
Mere Farm, Bridlington, East Yorkshire, YO25 3PT
www.bobbybee.co.uk

Quaint, quirky and rustic, this ramshackle camping ground with 'very free range' chickens roaming the site is a refreshing alternative to the mainstream campsites popping up everywhere in the UK. Located in the Yorkshire Wolds in the village of Burton Flemming and opposite a duck pond, the farm camp ground is in a perfect location for a Yorkshire village experience. The village itself has a local butcher's to stock up on your meat for BBQs, a post office and a pub serving food. Humanby Gap, a beautiful little family beach, is only three miles away from the site. If you venture to the pub at night or sup too much wine at your tent the 'Chuck Wagon' will cook up breakfast in a bun for you to take back to your tent and see the day in from your sleeping bag without the hassle of cooking breakfast for everyone.

Date:　　　　　Weather:　　　　　Your Rating: ☆ ☆ ☆ ☆ ☆

Notes:

KENDALL BANK FARM
Ripon, North Yorkshire, HG4 3QS
www.kendallbankfarm.com

Exclusive camping and party field for private rental in a secluded valley in Nidderdale, North Yorkshire. Based on a smallholding in one of Yorkshire's Areas of Outstanding Natural Beauty with beautiful views of the farm and the surrounding countryside, this makes a perfect escape for anyone wanting a private camping experience. Campfires are allowed and are even set up for your arrival if you hire the bell tent. If you are looking for somewhere to hold your own group camp this would be a perfect location; a marquee is even available. There is a wealth of things to do in the area, including visits to the Black Sheep and Theakston's breweries, or one of the courses available on the farm site. Learn how to make felt hats or slippers, and how to run your own smallholding and change your lifestyle.

▲ Date: ❄ Weather: ⚥ Your Rating: ☆ ☆ ☆ ☆ ☆

▲ Notes:

JOLLY DAYS LUXURY CAMPING
Village Farm, Scrayingham, North Yorkshire, YO41 1JD
www.jollydaysluxurycamping.co.uk

Jolly Days is the last word in luxury camping. If you are looking for an easy introduction to outdoor living and hate the thought of leaving your home comforts behind, then Jolly Days not only offers gorgeous lodge tents, fully equipped with all the essentials, but also fully kitted-out bell tents. Owners Carolyn and Christian van Outersterp have created a communal camping sanctuary in 200 acres of private woodland. With four-poster beds and a rolltop baths the luxury tents are more comfortable than some hotels. Only three hours from London in the stunning countryside of North Yorkshire this is a great weekend escape. Rydale, the York Moors, the coast and the Wolds are all on your doorstep, along with a great local farm shop and a variety of traditional Yorkshire pubs.

Date: Weather: Your Rating: ☆ ☆ ☆ ☆ ☆

Notes:

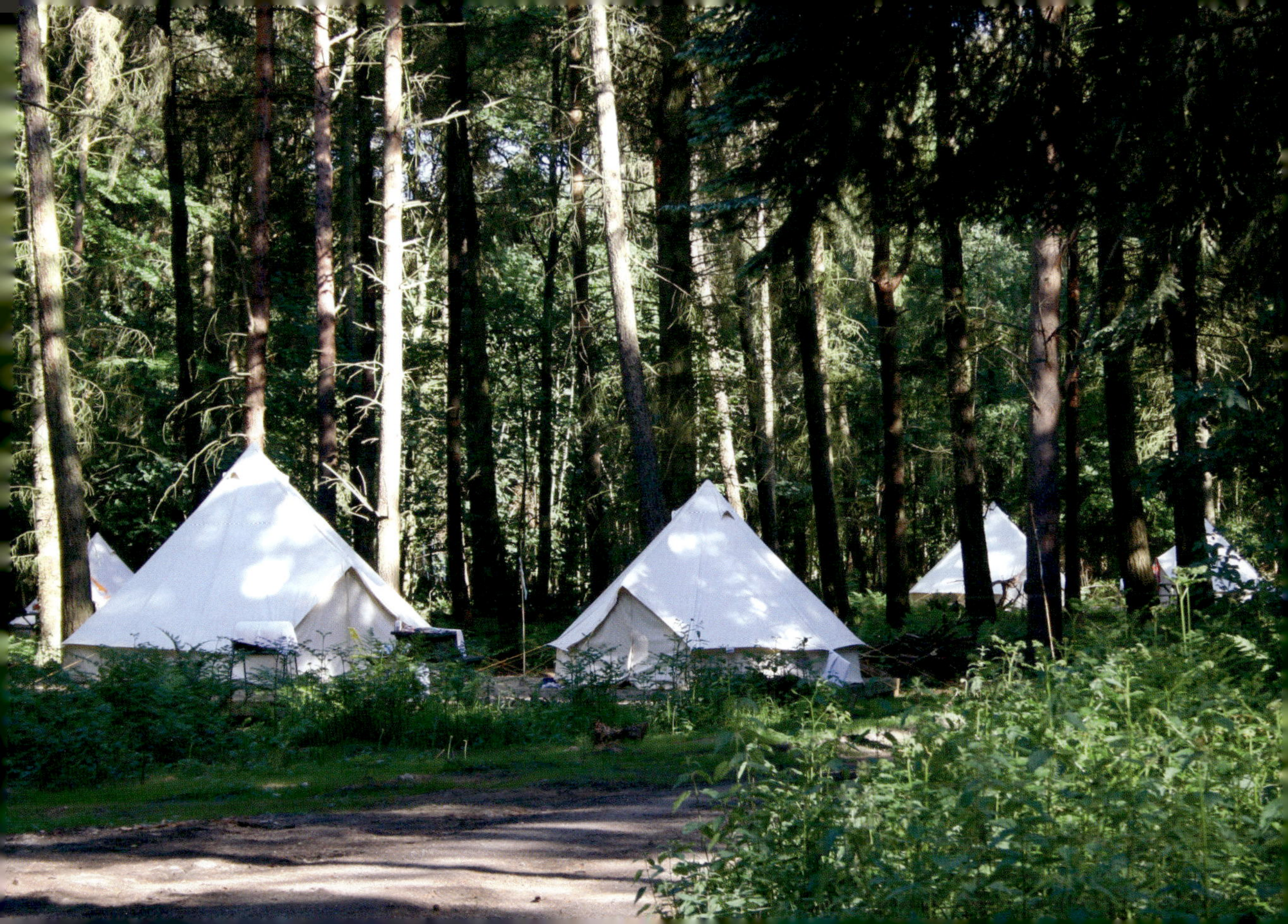

WHITBY SUNSET VIEW
Manor Farm, Normanby, Whitby, North Yorkshire, YO22 4PS
www.whitbysunsetview.co.uk

This site offers panoramic views of Whitby, the sea and the abbey across acres of fields; watch the lights of the town at night as the fishing boats come home, or the sun glinting off of the ocean during the day. The facilities are limited but the vista more than makes up for this and keeps the site from becoming completely overrun. Sunset View is a short drive or a bus trip to Whitby itself, and walking distance to a good local pub. Freshly cut hay bales are seasonably available to use as windbreakers, especially around the campfire, and are more often than not piled up by kids to climb over. During the summer you can take a trip on the Esk Valley Railway steam trains through the North Yorkshire National Park stopping in all the major Esk Valley villages.

▲ Date: ❄ Weather: ♙♙ Your Rating: ☆ ☆ ☆ ☆ ☆

▲ Notes:

HIGH YEDMANDALE FARM
West Ayton, Scarborough, North Yorkshire, YO13 9JZ

Rural camping only ten minutes from Scarborough. A hearty welcome is given to all by owners Ken and Isobel, who disallow group bookings, and resist over-filling the site to protect the sense of space and freedom the pitches enjoy. The camp is made up of acres of short-mown grass fields or putting-green pitches, perfect for running barefoot in the sun. Right next to one of the biggest forests in Yorkshire this site has an ancient feel and the trees give it character. High Yedmandale is now open all year for tent camping and would be a perfect location from which to photograph the changing seasons. With no marked-out pitches, if you have a larger family tent or want a secluded spot for your bell tent this site is perfect. A fantastic local pub, The Dennison, serves generous portions, and is only 2 miles away.

Date:

Weather:

Your Rating: ☆ ☆ ☆ ☆ ☆

Notes:

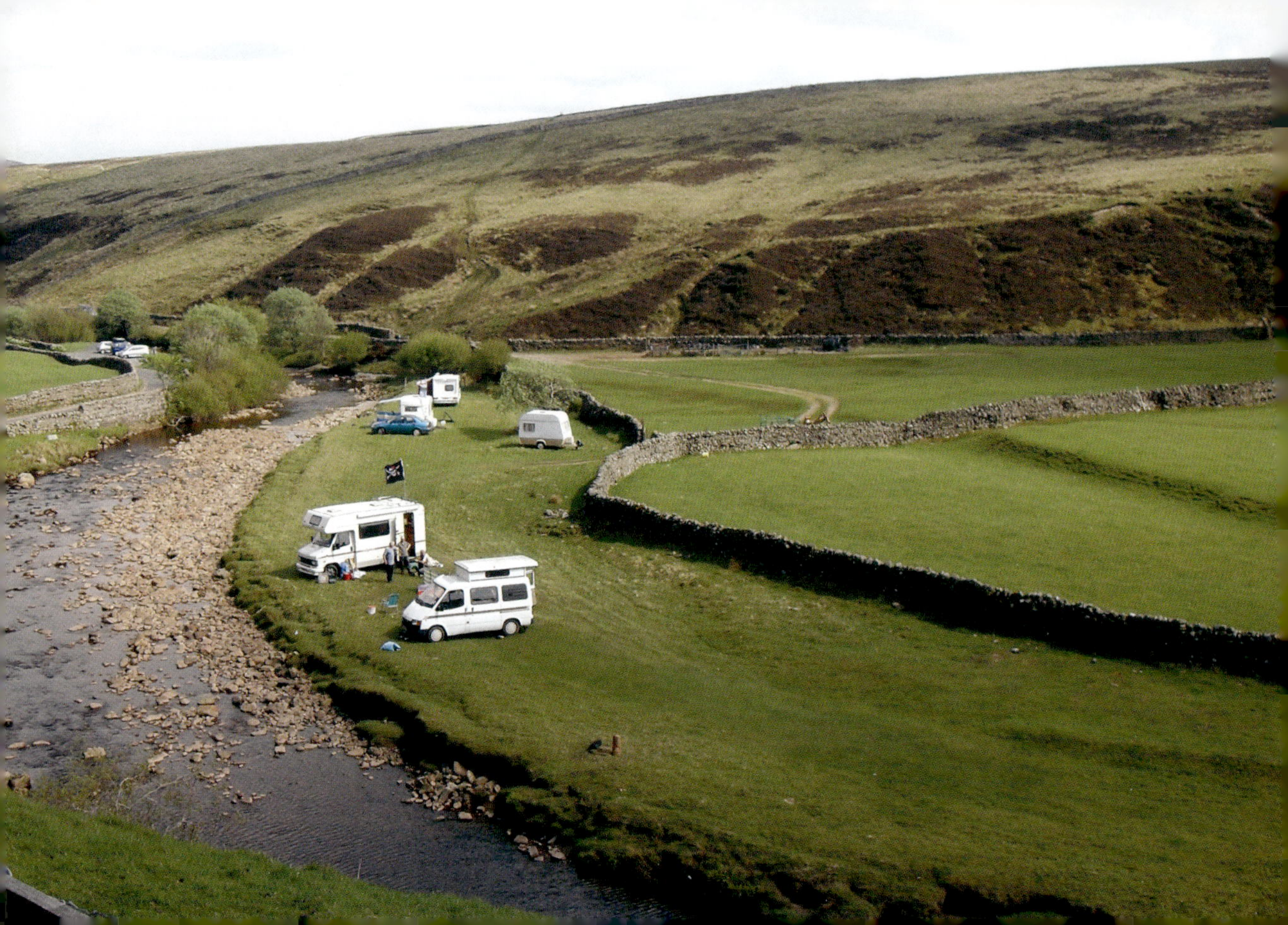

HOGGARTH'S FARM CAMPSITE
Keld, Richmond, North Yorkshire, DL11 6LT
www.swaledalecamping.co.uk

Wild camping pitches in the heart of the Swaledale in the Yorkshire Dales National Park, Hoggarth's Farm is a tiny campsite with no facilities but one that allows campfires and dogs. If you are looking to get away from it all and are brave enough to rough it then this pitch could be ideal for you. Water is available from the farmhouse but that is the extent of the facilities on offer. This area of Yorkshire is renowned for its outstanding scenery, crisscrossed by drystone walls and with stunning hay fields next to the dramatic moorland. There is a collection of four waterfalls around Keld, each with its own character, each more than worth a visit. Hoggarth's is a working farm and there may be an occasional sheep wandering onto the site to keep you company.

▲ Date: ❄ Weather: 👥 Your Rating: ☆ ☆ ☆ ☆ ☆

▲ Notes:

RUKIN'S CAMPSITE
Park Lodge, Keld, Richmond, North Yorkshire, DL11 6LJ
www.rukins-keld.co.uk

Rukin's is a great little campsite in which to get away from the outside world for a few days. Perched on the banks of the River Swale and allowing small campfires at the river's edge it enjoys an excellent location, ideal as a base for hiking and hill walking. Many visitors use Rukin's as an overnight stop on the Pennine Way. This is a good site for dog owners, as animals are allowed on site, but less ideal for 'groups of young adults', who aren't welcome. Take a dip in the river on warm days and watch the waterfalls as you munch on riverside picnics, but don't forget your insect repellant – Rukin's is popular with the midges, too. A wonderful little shop on site selling essentials, from red wine to burgers, and clean facilities make this place popular, so be sure to call ahead.

⛰ Date: ❄ Weather: 👥 Your Rating: ☆ ☆ ☆ ☆ ☆

⛰ Notes:

LANEFOOT FARM
Thornthwaite, Keswick, Cumbria, CA12 5RZ
www.stayinthornthwaite.co.uk

Situated between Bassenthwaite Lake and Derwent Water, Lanefoot Farm is an idyllic site with a choice of more sheltered meadow camping or an open field with views over Catbells, Skiddaw and Lord's Seat. It is perched beneath Whinlatter Forest and close to Thornthwaite village, where ospreys have been known to nest. This is a haven for bird lovers, walkers, cyclists and anyone with a desire to get back to nature. Lanefoot has the feel of a 'proper' campsite, allowing campfires for toasting marshmallows, with ducks, chickens and geese wandering around. A small shop on site sells free-range eggs and even jars of old-fashioned sweets. The campsite has basic facilities which help to keep it more natural and prevent it getting too busy; however, they are always clean and well stocked.

▲ Date: ✿ Weather: ♛ Your Rating: ☆ ☆ ☆ ☆ ☆

▲ Notes:

4 WINDS LAKELAND TIPIS

Low Ray Campsite, C/O 1 Barley Bridge, Staveley, Kendal, Cumbria, LA8 9PQ
www.4windslakelandtipis.co.uk

4 Winds is a pre-pitched tipi park located in the Low Ray National Trust Campsite in the beautiful Lake District. The tipi camp itself is within sight of Low Ray Castle, standing guard over Lake Windermere. The tipis are in a separate private area of the National Trust campsite, next to a river that flows into the lake, creating a secluded luxury camping area for you to completely relax in. There aren't many pitches where you can watch the mists roll off of vast lakeland waters from your own tipi, and follow it up with a cedar-scented hot shower while enjoying views of the forest and its wildlife. Visit Wray Castle itself and imagine Beatrix Potter in her youth dreaming up stories of Peter Rabbit and Tom Kitten in her summer visits to the castle.

Date: Weather: Your Rating: ☆ ☆ ☆ ☆ ☆

Notes:

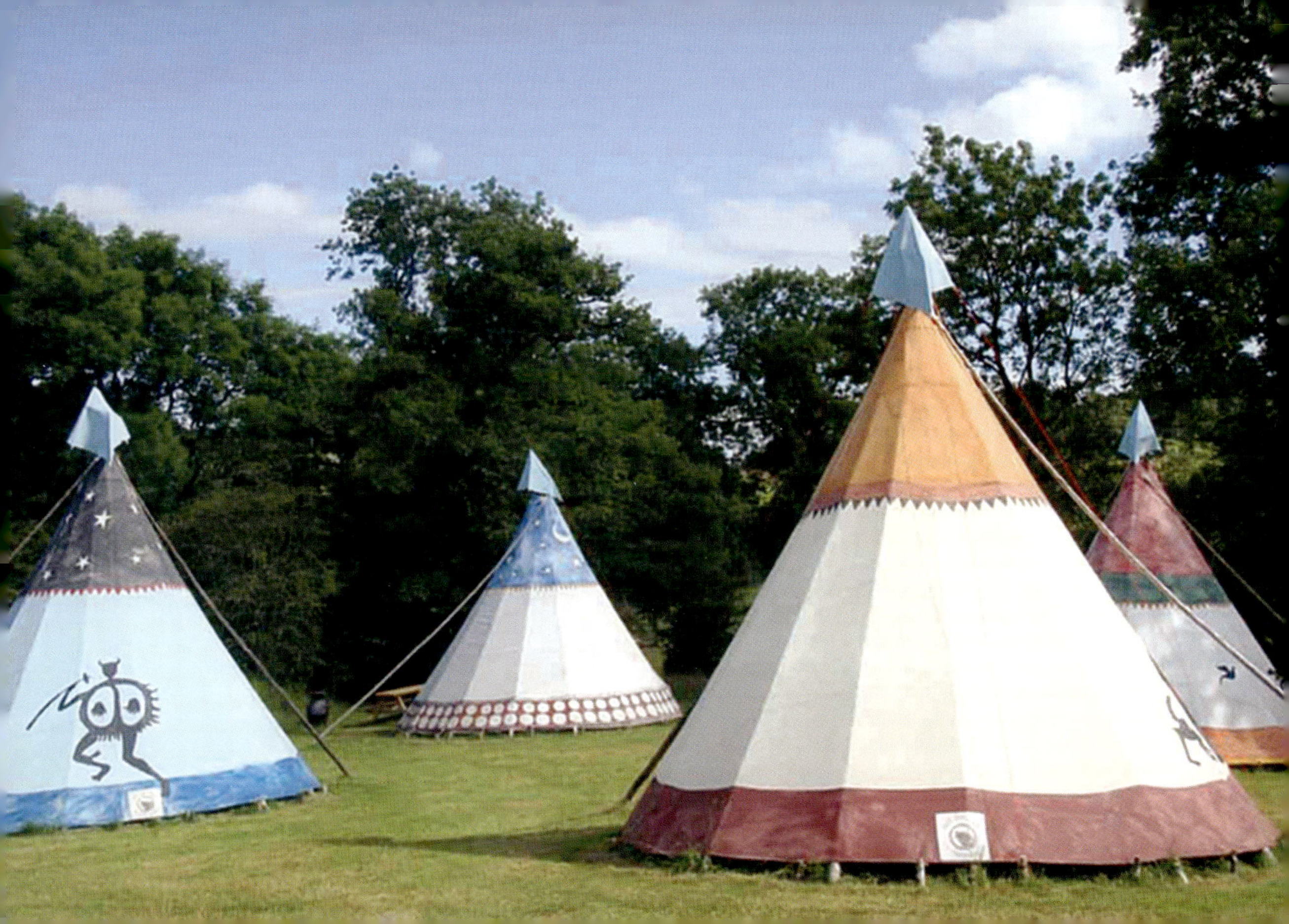

HOLME OPEN FARM
Sedbergh, Cumbria, LA10 5ET
www.holmeopenfarm.co.uk

An excellent camping field in a perfect location from which to tackle the three peaks. Holme Open Farm is a traditional Dales working farm with the added bonus of a camping field and café on site. The Ewe Tree Café serves homemade and locally-sourced food and would make a great pitstop for a cream tea on your way back to your tent after a long hike. The facilities are really basic and if you are looking for a quieter site this may not be ideal for you as this is a working farm and people tend to celebrate their walking achievements. A good social campsite! There is space to fish on the River Rawthey, and an evening badger watch is available by arrangement. No dogs allowed, though.

▲ Date: ☁ Weather: 👬 Your Rating: ☆ ☆ ☆ ☆ ☆

▲ Notes:

STONEHAUGH CAMPSITE
The Old Farmhouse, Stonehaugh, Hexham, Northumberland, NE48 3DZ

The beauty of Stonehaugh campsite is its situation, right in the centre of some of the most stunning woodland and countryside in the Northumberland National Park. If you feel like taking your bike and cycling around the area, the site is close to the National Cycle Route 68, stretching from Berwick-upon-Tweed to Appleby-in-Westmoorland in Cumbria. The nearest shops are in Wark which is 5 miles away. There are no other shops or pubs nearby, the only bar being that in a local social club in Stonehaugh. The peace and tranquillity wins over visitors to this area and they are charmed by the basic facilities and sense of serenity. The camp is powered by solar and wind power so leave the EHU behind and take in the silence; after all isn't that what camping is about?

▲ Date: ☼ Weather: ⚥ Your Rating: ☆ ☆ ☆ ☆ ☆

▲ Notes:

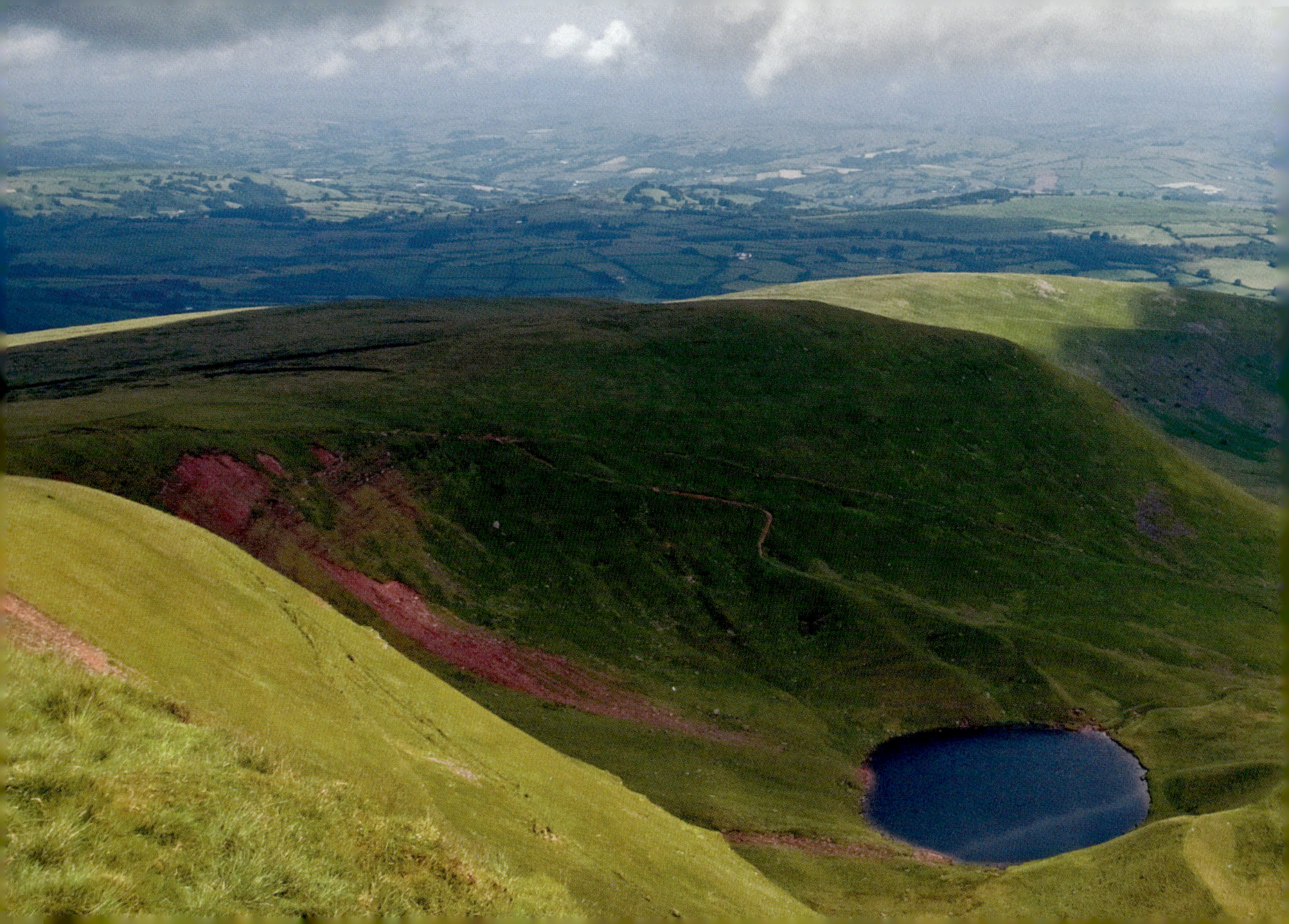

WALES

TRELLYN WOODLAND CAMPSITE
Abercastle, Pembrokeshire, SA62 5HJ
www.trellyn.co.uk

Trellyn is a peaceful little campsite in Pembrokeshire with just 5 pitches, 2 yurts, and 2 tipis. Set within a conservation ground and a stone's throw from rock pools for the children to hunt for crabs in, the camp is also near a coastal path with stunning sea views. Abbercastle is five minutes' walk away with its shops, coves and beaches. There is a choice of sheltered all-weather pitches, or grassland pitches amongst the woodland separated by a young labyrinth maze, or the meadow pitch furthest from the facilities. Each pitch has its own set of garden furniture and firewood all included in the price. Campfires are encouraged; cookware can be borrowed, and fresh lobster can be delivered by local fishermen for your evening cookout. Bushcraft days are also available if you fancy becoming the next Bear Grylls.

Date: Weather: Your Rating: ☆ ☆ ☆ ☆ ☆

Notes:

ARYMWNY
Mwny Hwnt, Abercastle, Pembrokeshire, SA62 5AL
www.campingwildwales.co.uk

As far away as possible from roads and towns, this pitch makes for good old-fashioned camping amongst several hundred acres of farmland. Arymwny is a wild camping experience but with the benefit of spotless flushing toilets, a fridge freezer for communal use and a shower room. You can pitch your tent in a meadow surrounded by wild flowers, rolling countryside and old field stones to build your own fire pit. This is a unique and outstandingly beautiful place to camp; or why not slumber in the tipi on this mystical Celtic hillside? Norman the owner welcomes you to enjoy his land with no curfew culture but with respect for the land itself. Getting back to nature is key on this camp site giving priority to the 'frogs in puddles, toads on roads, pheasants in fields, foxes on the forage, buzzards on poles...'

▲ Date: Weather: Your Rating: ☆ ☆ ☆ ☆ ☆

▲ Notes:

GLYN Y MUL FARM 'THE LONE WOLF CAMPSITE'
Aberdulais, Neath, West Glamorgan, SA10 8HF
www.glynymulfarm.co.uk

Hospitable and just big enough to cater for campers looking for a secluded and non-commercial site, Glyn Y Mul Farm is within easy reach of Gower and Swansea, making this a perfect little pitch. Set in 18 acres of woodland in which you can erect your tent, or even just a hammock, this is a great place to chill out after an active day exploring Gower and all it has to offer. As you cook your English (Welsh?) breakfast over the fire keep an eye out for herons on the pond and ducks waddling through camp. The woodland pitches are car free, wheelbarrows being available to lug your gear to your chosen plot, or a main camping field is available for those with more equipment. However 'lightweight' campers are encouraged and mountain bikers are welcomed.

▲ Date: ⛅ Weather: 👥 Your Rating: ☆ ☆ ☆ ☆ ☆

▲ Notes:

GLANGWY FARM
Llangruig, Llanidloes, Powys, SY18 6RS

Secluded and peaceful pitches in a small farm site tucked away in the countryside of the Wye Valley. The site consists of a couple of sheltered camping fields surrounded by trees and hedges with views of the surrounding valleys. In an area famous for its kite-spotting this site is an ideal space to sit back and watch the local wildlife pass you by. The owner lives in a bungalow across the lane and is more than helpful. Just a two minute walk from the farm is a beautiful little river where you can wade along its edge watching water washing through the shingle. The facilities here are basic; there are toilets and cold water taps, along with a shower at the main house, but the peace and tranquillity more than make up for this.

Date: Weather: Your Rating: ☆ ☆ ☆ ☆ ☆

Notes:

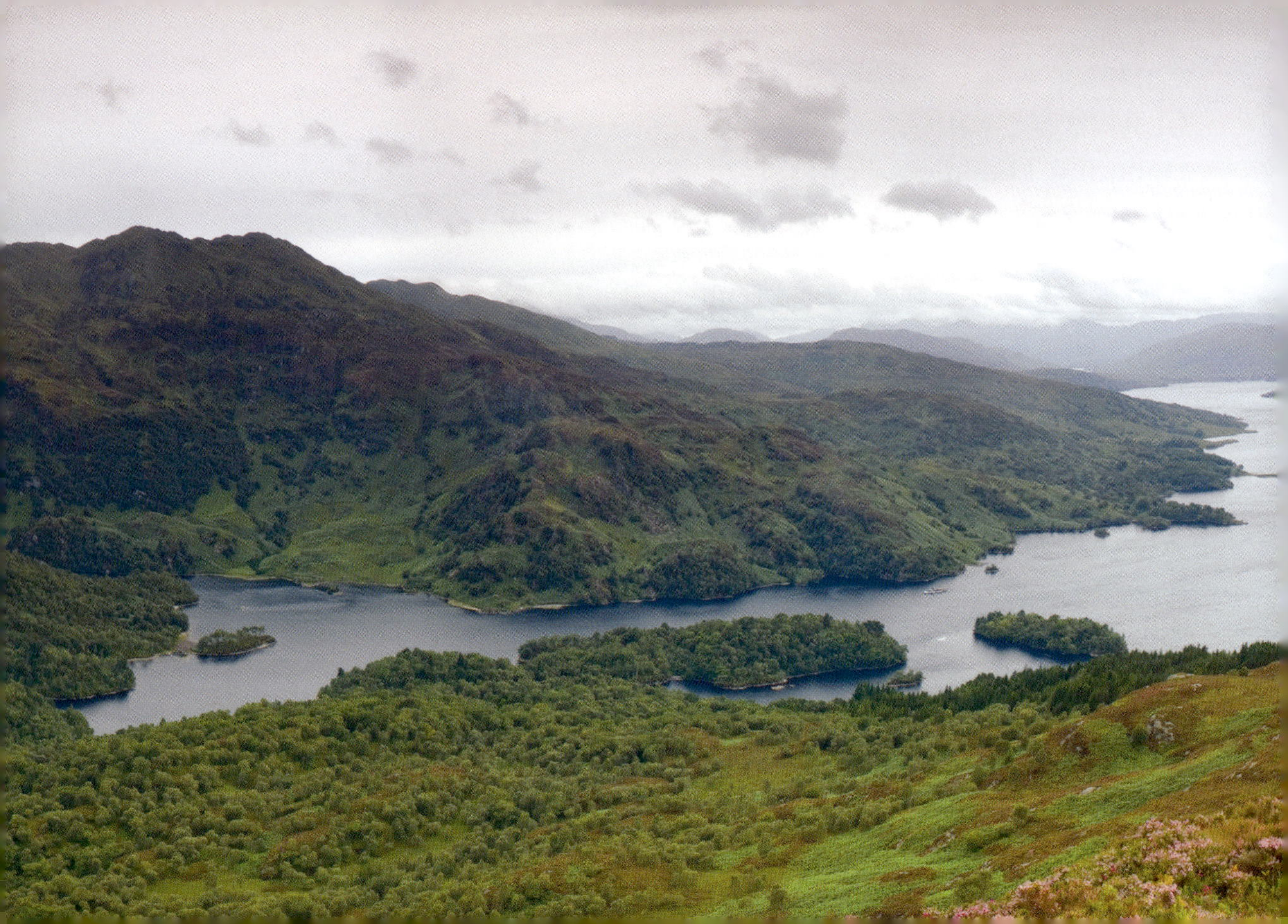

SCOTLAND & IRELAND

DULOCH HAMLET FIFE
2 Dales Farm Cottage, Inverkeithing, Dunfermline, Fife, KY11 7HR
www.camping-fife-near-edinburgh.blogspot.com

Quiet-ish children are welcome to bring well-behaved adults to this campsite. This is a quaint semi-wild site with individual clearings in woodland or meadows. The camp has a rustic charm with wild flowers, a herb garden and even a badger-watching hut. This is as far as you can get from busy overbooked campsites and has the limited facilities to reflect this. There is a compost toilet, a water point, and no showers but finishing touches like huge antique mirrors and tractor tyre tree swings give this campground a quirky appeal. Relax sitting round the crackling campfire at night as foxes and owls and other woodland creatures explore the forest. Edinburgh is only 10 miles away if you are thinking of attending the festival or heading to Murrayfield for the rugby.

▲ Date: ❄ Weather: ⛺ Your Rating: ☆ ☆ ☆ ☆ ☆

▲ Notes:

GLEN ROSA
Glen Sherraig House, Glen Rosa, Isle of Arran, Scotland, KA27 8DF
www.glenrosa.com

Spacious and exceptionally beautiful, Glen Rosa is sited next to the Glen Rosa track which leads to the Arran Hills, including the highest peak, Goatfell. With Rosa Burn running through the campground the site is a mecca for midges so make sure you are fully prepared with insect repellent and a good campfire. Extremely basic facilities so not ideal for families but perfect for keen hill walkers as you can literally start out from your tent flap after breakfast. Fishing permits can be bought if you are planning an angling trip. The access to this site makes it difficult for anyone without a 4x4 so it is a perfect site for anyone looking to backpack or cycle. However this really is a unique site with a majestic view so is worth considering.

A Date: Weather: Your Rating: ☆ ☆ ☆ ☆ ☆

A Notes:

SANGO SANDS OASIS
Durness, Highlands, IV27 4PP
www.sangosands.com

Travelling to Sango Sands makes you feel as if you are in a totally different part of the world. The landscape is like nowhere else in Great Britain, breathtaking and remote, with stunning white beaches and rocky mountains giving a sense of true isolation. The clifftop camping ground of Sango Sands is not for the faint-hearted, perched as it is on weather-beaten cliffs overlooking the dramatic coastline. The campers' kitchen on site is a communual area fit to shelter in if the weather takes a turn for the worse. Good tent pegs, all-weather gear and a sense of adventure are vital. With a restaurant and craft village there is enough in this location to keep you entertained for a few days but the site really is for outdoor enthusiasts who are capable of looking after themselves

▲ Date: ☁ Weather: 👫 Your Rating: ☆ ☆ ☆ ☆ ☆

▲ Notes:

RED SQUIRREL CAMPSITE
Argyll, Scotland, PH49 4HX
www.redsquirrelcampsite.co.uk

Camping as nature intended. Relaxed and easy-going set alongside the River Coe, this site is perfect if you are looking for somewhere to indulge in a spot of wild swimming at the foot of the mountains. The site itself is wooded and therefore sheltered with a natural swimming hole for cooling off in. There are 22 acres of camping so the site has a wilder feel to it, one of the reasons why people have been camping here since 1914. If you are a keen angler then permit fishing is allowed on the river. A perfect location for touring all of Scotland, only a mile and a half from the nearest village and a mile to the local pub, the Glachaig Inn. Campfires are allowed but have to be extinguished after 11pm. Pitch your tent against a stunning backdrop of dramatic mountainous scenery.

▲ Date: ❄ Weather: 👥 Your Rating: ☆ ☆ ☆ ☆ ☆

▲ Notes:

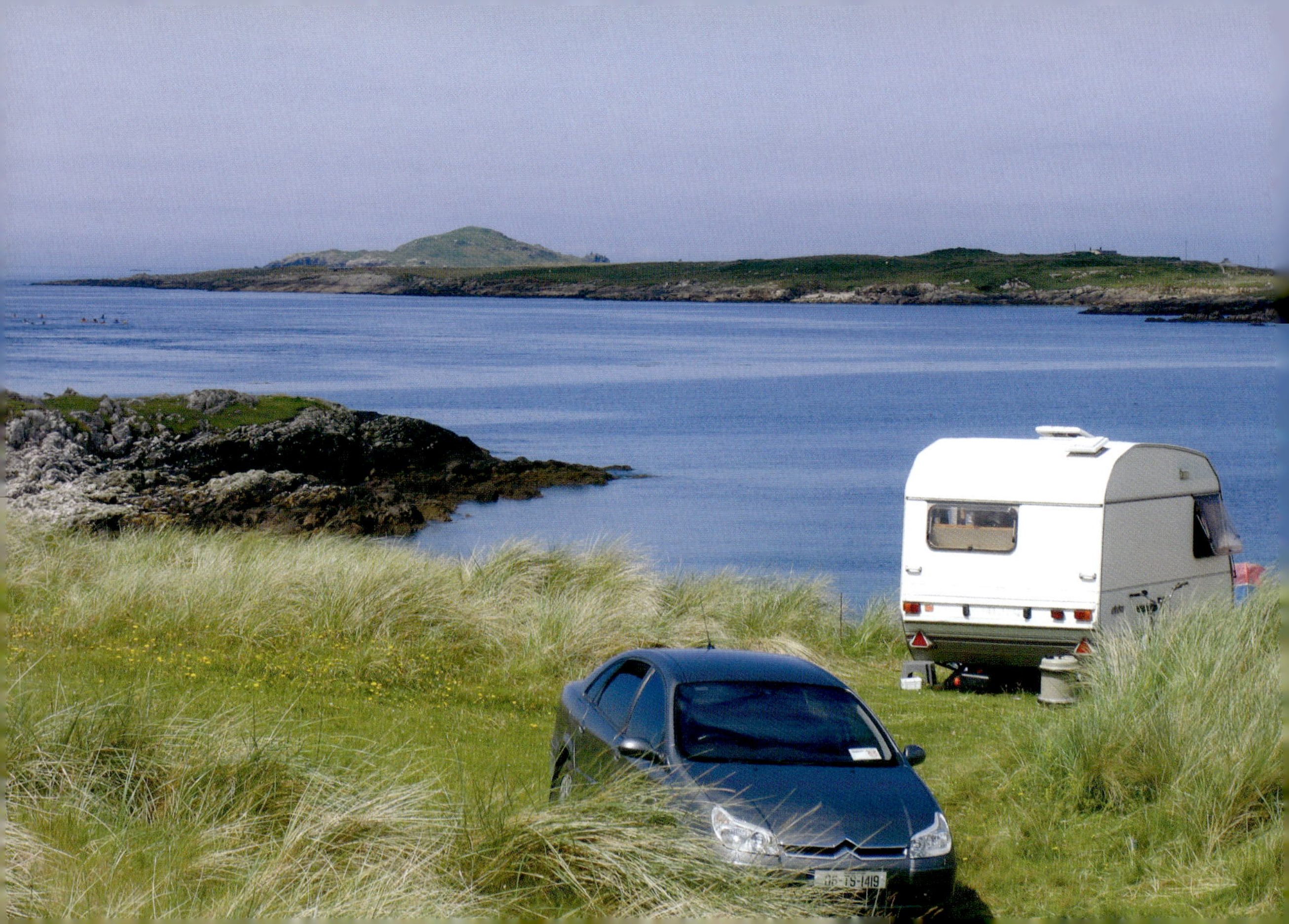

ACTON'S BEACHSIDE CARAVAN & CAMPING PARK
Claddaghduff, Clifton, Co. Galway
www.actonsbeachsidecamping.com

Perched on a small peninsula where a stream meets the Atlantic Ocean, this is a truly special wild camping plot, an organic farm set amongst the sand dunes with spectacular seascape views of the surrounding islands and mountains. Acton's is located on the wilder west coast of Galway and is a great location for families with a love of the outdoors. In fact, anyone looking for a wilder camp but with good facilities will fall in love with this quiet location, with its own spring for totally natural water and direct access to a lovely white sand beach – what more could you ask for? Dine on local oysters, catch your own mackerel, cook it over the campfire and raise a thankful pint of Guinness.

▲ Date: ☒ Weather: ☗ Your Rating: ☆ ☆ ☆ ☆ ☆

▲ Notes:

CLACHTOLL BEACH CAMPSITE
Clachtoll, Lochinver, Highlands, IV27 4JD
www.clachtollbeachcampsite.co.uk

Coastal camping in a small family-run beachside touring caravan and camping site. Clachtoll sits perched above the shore nestled between sandy and rocky beaches, surrounded by diverse landscapes from boggy moorland to dramatic sea cliffs just 5 miles north of Lochinver, where you can pick up your provisions from the local shops. A vacation in this area can be as active or as relaxed as you want it to be but there is a huge variety of activities on offer: caving, sea kayaking, and cliff jumping for the more adventurous, or for a more gentle introduction to the local area explore the lochs, cycle past traditional croft houses, visit spectacular waterfalls or go sailing to spot dolphins, basking sharks, whales and seals. The ground on this site is very soft so it's a perfect place to pitch your tent.

Date: **Weather:**   **Your Rating:** ☆ ☆ ☆ ☆ ☆

Notes:

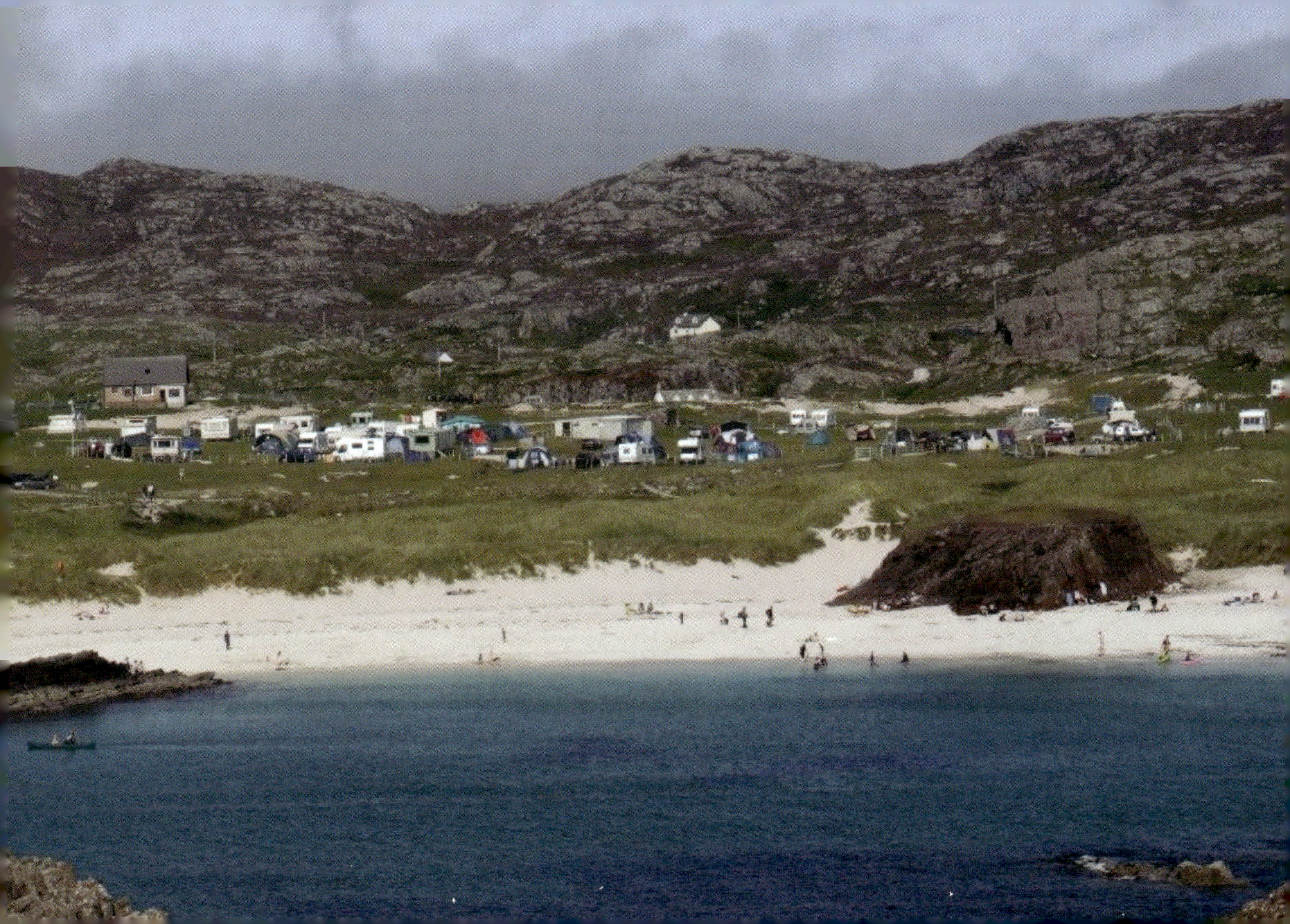

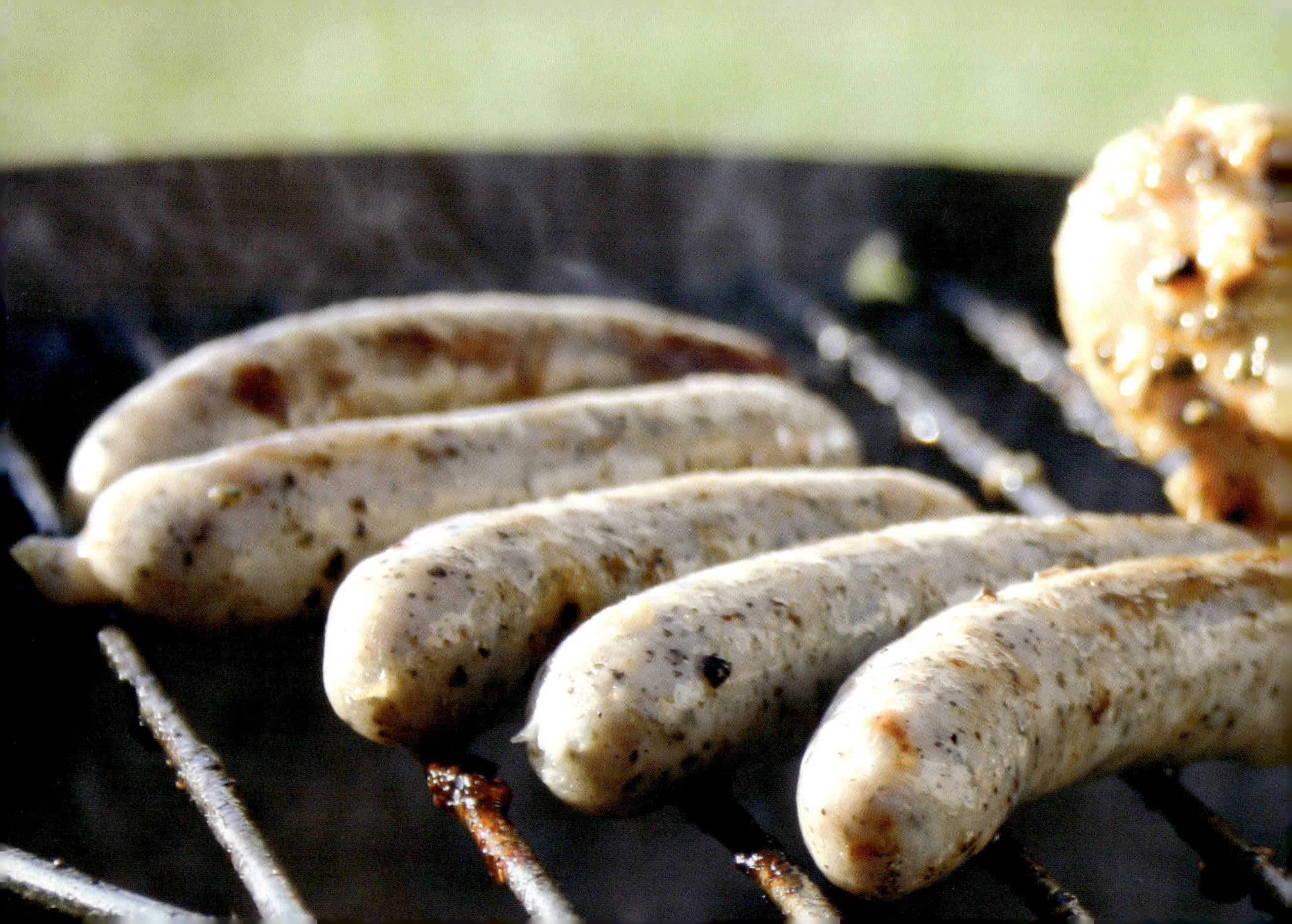

CAMP COOKERY

RECIPES

Mint & Chilli Lamb Burgers with Greek Salad

Some of the best camping memories are of sitting in the sun drinking rosé wine as we tuck in to a gorgeous fresh Greek salad and these lamb burgers perfectly compliment the feta in the salad. If you want a heartier meal tuck the burgers into slightly toasted buns or French bread with the salad added on top of the burger, or as a side dish. Cook the burgers on a BBQ or grill over your campfire, but they can also just as easily be fried on a camping stove or cooked on a party grill.

Ingredients (serves 4)

Mint & Chilli Lamb Burgers

600g lean lamb mince (preferably from a local butcher)

1 small onion, finely diced

3 tbsp fresh mint, chopped

1 tbsp dried oregano
1 tsp dried chili flakes
Salt and pepper to season

Greek Salad

1 large red onion, finely chopped
Half a cucumber, finely chopped
200g feta cheese, cut into small cubes
1 beef tomato, finely chopped
6 tbsp olive oil
juice of 1 lemon
Some fresh pitted olives

Method

In a large bowl mix together the mince, onion, mint, chilli, oregano and seasoning. Divide into four equal portions and create four patties. Cook on the grill, turning half way through with a spatula, ensuring that the burgers don't fall apart. Cook for roughly five minutes on each side, until the burger is cooked through to your liking.

In a separate bowl mix together all of the ingredients for the salad. Once the burgers are cooked, serve with the salad, along with burger buns or bread if desired.

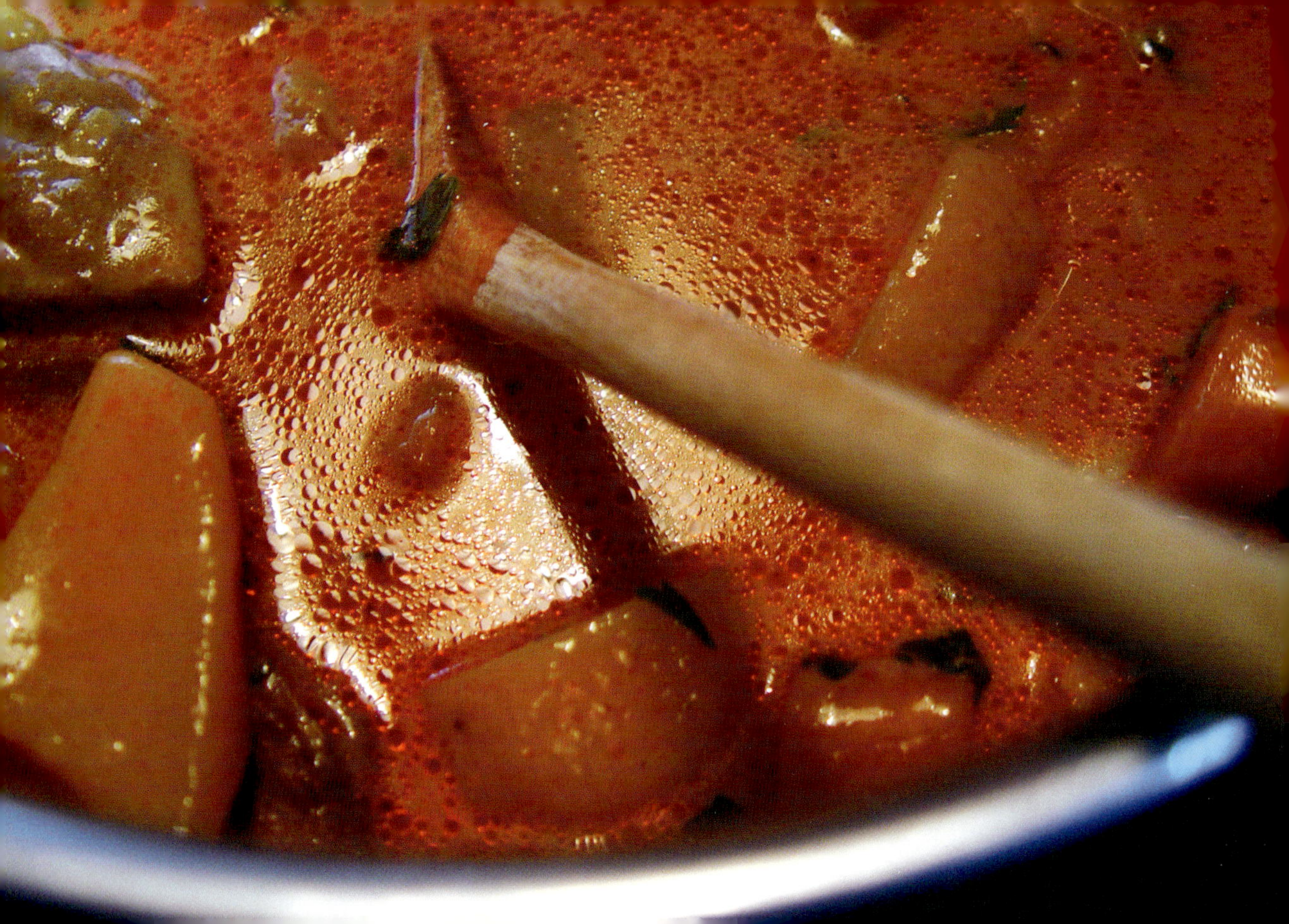

Jamaican Jerk Chicken, Rice and Beans, and Mango and Lime Salsa

Everything about this recipe is delicious. It sounds amazing, smells great, is easy to prepare and tastes fantastic. Simply marinated chicken grilled on a BBQ or cooked in a skillet, served with Dutch Oven-cooked rice and beans with a tangy salsa. The smell of this cooking makes my mouth water every time.

Ingredients (serves 4)

Jerk Chicken

4 boneless chicken breasts, skin on
4 tbsp jerk seasoning
2 tbsp light soy sauce
6 tbsp tomato ketchup
2 tbsp clear honey
1 tbsp olive oil
A pinch of ground black pepper

Rice and Beans

50g butter
4 spring onions, finely chopped
2 shallots, finely chopped
2 garlic cloves, peeled and crushed
200ml light coconut milk
200g brown basmati rice
410g can kidney beans (do not drain)

2 fresh thyme sprigs
1 tsp salt
620ml boiling water
1 Scotch bonnet pepper, whole

Mango, Green Pepper and Lime Salsa

1 large ripe mango
Half a red onion, finely chopped
1 green pepper, finely chopped
Half a red chilli, deseeded and finely chopped
3 tbsp fresh coriander, chopped
Zest and juice of one lime
3 tbsp olive oil
A pinch of black pepper

Rice and Beans

Place the Dutch oven on a tripod over the fire. Melt the butter in the oven and fry the spring onions, shallots and garlic until softened, adding a little water if needed to prevent burning. Add the coconut milk and gently bring to the boil, stirring continuously.

Next add the rice, along with the kidney beans, thyme, salt and boiling water. Once this is simmering again add the whole Scotch bonnet, stir thoroughly, and replace the oven lid, bringing the liquid back to the boil. Once the liquid is boiling again raise the Dutch oven slightly and allow to simmer over the fire for 30–40 minutes, until all of the liquid is absorbed into the rice and it is cooked through. Keep stirring and checking to make sure it doesn't stick or burn. Once cooked, take off of the fire and keep the lid on to keep warm.

Jerk Chicken

Score the skin of the chicken breasts with a sharp knife and place to one side whilst you mix the marinade. In a small mixing bowl stir together the jerk seasoning, soy sauce, tomato ketchup, honey, black pepper and olive oil to create a paste. Brush half of the marinade over the chicken breasts and keep the second half for basting during grilling.

If you are cooking on the BBQ make sure the coals are white and generating an even heat once the flames have died down before you cook the chicken. Place the chicken on the grill or skillet and cook slowly turning halfway through, and base with the rest of the marinade as you cook the meat. Cook until the skin is crispy and cooked through. This should take about 25–30 minutes.

Mango, Green Pepper and Lime Salsa

Peel the mango, and remove the central stone by slicing the mango in half. Dice into small chunks and place in the serving bowl. Next mix the mango pieces with the red onion, green pepper, chilli and coriander. Finally add the lime juice, zest and olive oil, and season to flavour with the salt and pepper.

When the chicken is cooked through, serve with the rice and a side helping of salsa.

Perfect Jacket Potatoes

Campfire cooked jacket potatoes taste so homely, and are a delicious accompaniment to any meal, or can be served on their own. If you have a microwave on the campsite you may want to cook the potatoes for 10 minutes first (before adding the oil and salt and pepper) to give them a good start and then cook for half an hour in the fire to crisp up the skins in the tin foil. For a hint of spice add a few dried chilli flakes along with the salt and pepper.

Ingredients (serves 4)

4 large jacket potatoes

Olive oil

Salt and pepper

Butter to serve

Tin foil

Method

Pierce the potato skins with a fork or knife. Tear four sheets of tin foil, large enough to cover each potato. Place a splash of olive oil on each sheet and rub in to the potato skin. Cover with salt and pepper and wrap up in the foil.

Place the potatoes in the embers of your campfire, ensuring they are away from the flames. Cook for around an hour in the fire, turning occasionally to make sure they do not burn and are evenly cooked. When the skins are crispy and the potatoes soft inside, remove from the foil with oven gloves and cut open, serving with a delicious helping of butter.

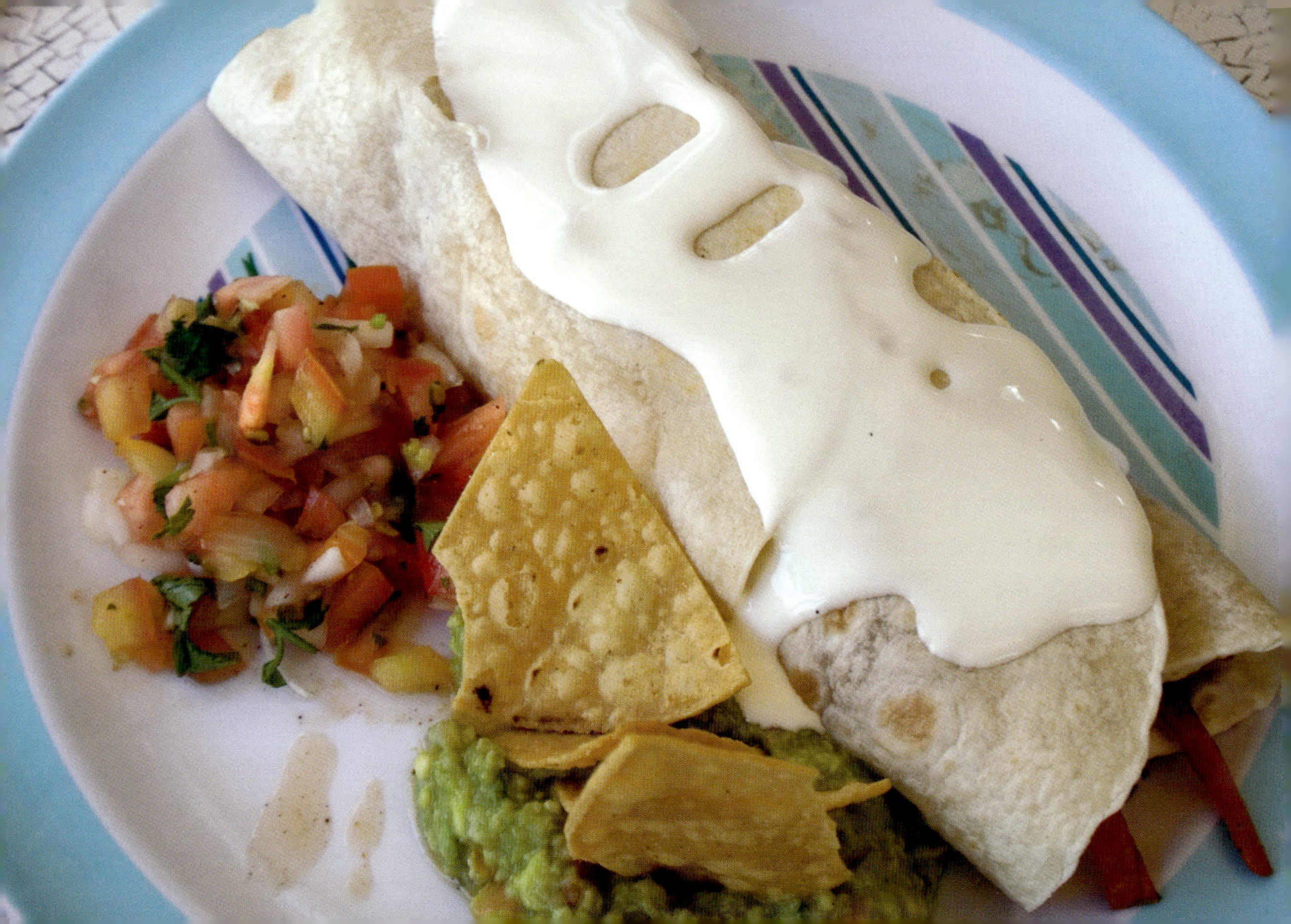

Spicy Chorizo and Potatoes with Mediterranean Fire Roasted Vegetable and Halloumi Kebabs

This is a wonderful combination of Mediterranean foods to cook over the campfire using a large skillet and skewers. Use the logs of the fire to create a level cooking space above the flames or spread some of the embers to the front of the fire and place the skillet directly into the heat. Make sure you keep the fire going to ensure adequate cooking time.

Ingredients

Spicy Chorizo and Potatoes
1 onion, finely chopped
6 medium/large potatoes, peeled and sliced
2 garlic cloves, sliced
2 chorizo cooking sausages, sliced
1 litre chicken stock
Olive oil for frying

Vegetable and Halloumi Kebabs
250g halloumi cheese
1 red onion
2 red peppers
100g mushrooms
200g cherry tomatoes
1 tbsp olive oil
1 tsp mixed herbs (fresh if available)

Method

Cut the halloumi, red onion, and red peppers into large chunks. Mix these along with the mushrooms and tomatoes in a large bowl and add the olive oil and herbs, making sure they are all mixed in well. Alternately thread the cheese and vegetables onto the skewers and set aside for cooking later on.

Heat the olive oil in the skillet and fry the slices of chorizo until they are browned. Remove and place on a separate plate. Add the onions and garlic to the skillet and fry until golden, adding a little water to prevent sticking to the pan. Once they are cooked through, remove from the pan and add to the plate with the chorizo.

Add a little more oil to the pan and heat. Add the sliced potatoes and brown for a few minutes. Add the chicken stock and gently boil the potatoes. When the potatoes are tender add the onion, garlic and chorizo and leave over the heat for five minutes to heat through and ensure the flavours mix together.

As the potatoes and chorizo cook in the skillet, grill the kebabs over the fire until the cheese turns golden and the vegetables are slightly charred.

Vegetarian Burritos and Salami Quesadillas with Salsa

One of my favourite foods at a festival is a vegetarian burrito, the best ones being from The End Of The Road Festival. The festival is right at the end of the season and you really need to keep yourself warm; if you are feeling the cold just add extra chillies to spice it up and wash it down with cider. Quesadillas are also a great little campsite treat, as they need very little cooking and are a great snack to cook for your friends whilst you are setting up your festival or camping pitch. These can be cooked on a gas stove, over a campfire, or at home and served in your garden.

Ingredients (serves 4)

Vegetable Burritos

435g tin of refried beans
250g pre-cooked brown rice
1 jalapeno chilli chopped
Juice of one lime
110g tin of black-eyed beans, drained

4 flour tortillas
2 spring onions, roughly chopped
3 tsp coriander, roughly chopped
1 tbsp olive oil
A pinch of black pepper

Salami Quesadillas

8 flour tortillas

250g emmental cheese

Half a red onion, sliced

1 jalapeno chilli, very finely chopped

300g sliced salami

Salsa

150g tinned sweetcorn, drained

20g chillies, very finely chopped

Juice of one lime

2 tbsp coriander, chopped

1 red onion, finely chopped

200g cherry tomatoes, quartered

Method

Vegetarian Burrito

Add the olive oil to a pre-heated saucepan. Once the oil and pan are hot add the chopped spring onion and cook until it starts to brown, stirring frequently. Add the pre-cooked rice, heating it through and gently adding a little water if it starts to stick to the bottom of the pan. Season as necessary.

Add the rest of the ingredients apart from the tortillas, and heat for 10 minutes until piping hot. Warm the tortillas for a minute in the skillet, turning over regularly to make sure they don't burn.

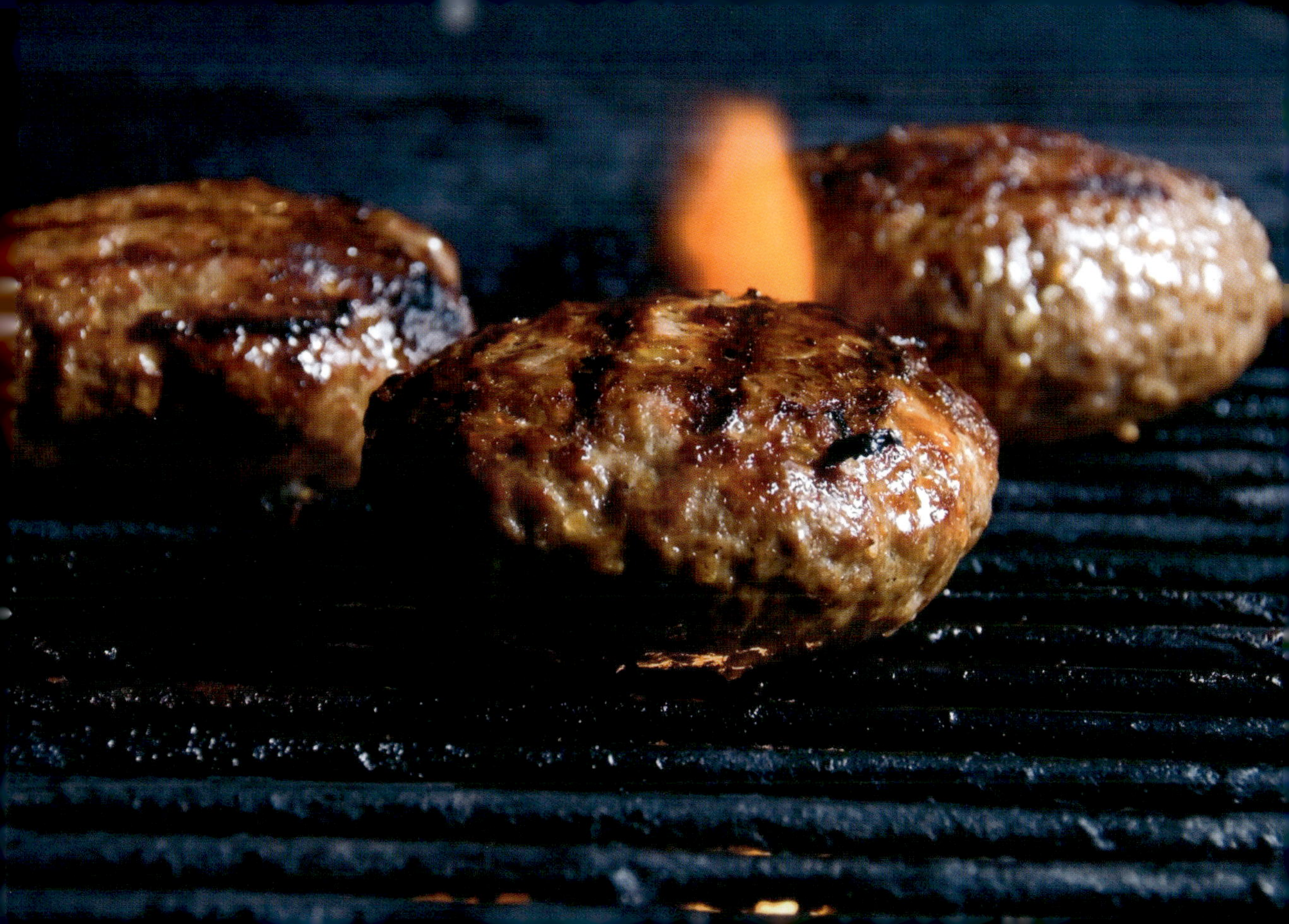

When you are ready place the tortillas on a plate, the vegetarian mixture in a bowl, and serve with the salsa allowing people to create their own burrito by wrapping the mixture inside the tortilla, folding in the ends to keep it together.

Salami Quesadillas

Place a tortilla flat on a plate, and layer a quarter of the salami, onion slices, chilli and cheese on top of it. Place another tortilla on top. Place in a heated skillet and cook for two minutes, turning halfway through in order to melt the cheese and seal the two tortillas together. Repeat with the rest of the ingredients to make three more. Slice each quesadilla into quarters and serve with the salsa and burritos.

Salsa

Simply mix all of the ingredients together in a bowl and serve alongside the burritos and quesadillas.

Perfect Pitch Banoffee Pie

This pudding recipe was passed down to me by a family friend. When I was 15 he made this at a BBQ at our house, and my family have been making it ever since. You can prepare the toffee sauce the night before you go to make things easier, but do remember to take a round cake dish with you in order to make the pie on site. It still tastes as fantastic as it did all those years ago. Just watch out when you dish it up as all your camping neighbours may become your new best friends.

Ingredients (serves 8)

400g tin condensed milk
2 bananas
284ml double cream or whipping cream
1 chocolate flake
1 tsp instant coffee powder (this can be left out) mixed with a drop of warm water to dissolve the powder

1 pre-baked sweet pastry case (or you can make your own)

Method

The night before

Fill a small saucepan with boiling water. Place the unopened can of condensed milk in the saucepan so that it is completely covered. Simmer for 3 hours, making sure that the water doesn't boil away, topping up with more water if necessary.

Take the tin out of the water using tongs and put to one side to cool down overnight. Be careful to place it on a heatproof surface.

You also have the choice of making things even easier for yourself by buying a can of Dulce de Leche caramel, therefore saving yourself the task of boiling the condensed milk. If you are baking your own pastry case make sure you cook it the night before so that it is cold when you travel, as it will be less likely to crumble.

On site

Put the ready-made pastry case in the bottom of the cake tin. Slice the bananas thinly and layer them evenly on the bottom of the pastry case.

In a bowl, mix the double cream with the coffee powder (if you are using it), and whip it until it stands in stiff peaks.

Open the tin of condensed milk which will now be a thick caramel, and pour it over the bananas. Spread it evenly so that it covers the base. Pour the whipped cream over the caramel. Crush the chocolate flake and sprinkle it over the cream. You can either serve it up straight away or leave it to cool.

Orange Peel and Sultana Drop Scones with Maple Syrup

Delicious drop scones cooked on the campfire in a skillet served with a generous helping of maple syrup makes a great breakfast or pudding. They not only taste great but also look fantastic and smell amazing as they cook. To make it easier for yourself mix the batter in advance and store in an airtight container and keep it cooled ready for when you need it. If you don't fancy cooking these on the campfire then you could just use a normal camping stove and a frying pan. You could also use alternative dried fruits such as cranberries or apricots. For a savoury meal, leave out the fruit and sugar and serve the scones with scrambled eggs and bacon.

Ingredients

250g plain flour

1 tsp baking powder

25g caster sugar

Pinch of salt

2 eggs

25g butter, melted

250ml milk

50g dried fruit (sultanas or raisins)

25g orange peel

Butter for frying

Method

Sift the flour, baking powder, salt and sugar into a mixing bowl. Add the eggs, beating after each addition. Add the milk, beating frequently, then drizzle in the melted butter. When you have a thick and creamy batter, add the dried fruit and orange peel. If you are preparing the batter in advance don't add the dried fruit and orange peel until you are on site. You're now ready to start cooking.

Melt a little butter in the skillet (or frying pan) and then drop a large dollop of batter into the pan. The mixture will flatten as it cooks. Let the batter cook until it turns golden on one side, then flip it and cook the other side. Serve drizzled with a helping of maple syrup.